MACMILLAN EXAMS

# Ready for CAE

## workbook

Roy Norris

Amanda French

Suitable for the updated CAE exam

Macmillan Education
Between Towns Road, Oxford OX4 3PP
A division of Macmillan Publishers Limited
Companies and representatives throughout the world

ISBN 978-0-2300-2888-3 (+key edition)
ISBN 978-0-2300-2889-0 (-key edition)



First published 2008



Designed by eMC Design; www.emcdesign.org.uk
Illustrated by Richard Duszczak, Peter Harper and Laszlo Veres
Cover design by Barbara Mercer
Cover photograph by Corbis

We would like to thank Joe Wilson, Deborah Friedland, Amanda Anderson and Louise Tester for their excellent editorial work. Roy Norris would also like to thank his wife, Azucena, and daughters, Lara and Elisa, for their support and understanding. Amanda French would like to thank Liam Keane, and staff at Languages International, Auckland.

The publishers would like to thank Paulette Dooler, Permissions Consultant for all her hard work in obtaining text permissions for this course.

The author and publishers are grateful for permission to reprint the following copyright material: Extract from 'Is this your idea of fun?' by Mark MacKenzie copyright © The Independent 2004, first published in *The Independent* 11.02.04, reprinted by permission of the publisher.
Extracts from 'Island Hopping to a New World' by Alex Markels copyright © U.S News & World Report 2004, first published in *US News & World Report* 23.02.04, reprinted by permission of the publisher.
Extract from 'The house of maps' by Peter Whitfield from *Geographical* Magazine December 2003, reprinted by permission of the publisher.
Extract from 'No cure for the summertime blues' by Paul Gould copyright © Paul Gould 2003, first published in *Financial Times* 06.09.03. reprinted by permission of the author.
Extract from 'Ring for Mrs Jeeves' by Kate Spicer copyright © N I Syndication 2002, first published in *The Sunday Times* 01.09.02, reprinted by permission of the publisher.
Extract from 'A daily hug brings the touch of success' by Oliver Wright copyright © N I Syndication 2002, first published in *The Times* 05.04.02, reprinted by permission of the publisher.
Extract from 'Machine rage is dead... long live emotional computing: consoles and robots detect and respond to users' feelings' by Robin McKie copyright © Guardian News & Media Limited 2004, first published in *The Observer* 11.04.04, reprinted by permission of the publisher.
Extract from *The Kitchen God's Wife* by Amy Tan (Fontana, 1991) copyright © Amy Tan 1991, reprinted by permission of Harper Collins and Abner Stein.
Extract from 'Dutch freedom and respect allow youth to flourish' by Isabel Conway copyright © The Independent 2007, first published in *The Independent* 14.02.07, reprinted by permission of the publisher.
Extract from 'Paws for thought' by Mary Braid copyright © N I Syndication 2004, first published in *The Sunday Times* 01.02.04, reprinted by permission of the publisher.
Extract from 'Noises after hours' by Luisa Dillner copyright © Guardian News & Media Limited 1996, first published in *The Guardian* 23.01.96, reprinted by permission of the publisher.
Extract from 'Musical genius is genetic, twins study shows' by David Charter copyright © N I Syndication 2001, first published in *The Times* 09.03.01, reprinted by permission of the publisher.
Extract from 'The boy who broke every rule in the book' by Scarlett Thomas copyright © The Independent 2004, first published in *The Independent* 29.02.04, reprinted by permission of the publisher.
Extract from 'The new way to burn fat – set yourself on fire' by Hazel Knowles copyright © The Telegraph 2005, first published in *The Sunday Telegraph* 05.12.05, reprinted by permission of the publisher.
Extract from 'It's so easy to work out' by Wanda Cash copyright © The Telegraph 2003, first published in *The Daily Telegraph* 06.02.03, reprinted by permission of the publisher.
Extract from 'The Truth is out There on the Net' by Clive Thompson copyright © Clive Thompson 2004, taken from *The New Zealand Herald* 05.04.04.
Extract from 'Mobile throwing contest is too close to call' by Tim Moore copyright © N I Syndication 2002, first published in *The Times* 23.08.02, reprinted by permission of the publisher.
Extract from 'Driving in New Zealand' taken from *www.newzealand.com*, reprinted by permission of the publisher.
Extract from *The Art of Travel* by Alain de Botton (Hamish Hamilton, 2002) copyright © Alain de Botton 2002, reprinted by permission of Penguin Books Ltd.
Extract from 'Wide Angle National Geographical Western and Southern Europe' edited by Ferdinand Protzman (National Geographic, 2005), reprinted by permission of the publisher.
Extract from 'Dear luggage wish you were here...' by Mark Hodson copyright © N I Syndication 2002, first published in *The Sunday Times* 28.08.02, reprinted by permission of the publisher.
Extract from 'The revolution in the way we travel' by Simon Calder copyright © The Independent 2007, first published in *The Independent* 15.06.07, reprinted by permission of the publisher.
Extract from 'Social climbers build new life in treetops' by Tom Robbins and Geraldine Murray copyright © N I Syndication 2000, first published in *The Sunday Times* 13.02.00, reprinted by permission of the publisher.
Extract from 'My Paris' copyright © The Independent 2004, first published in *The Independent on Sunday* 21.03.04, reprinted by permission of the publisher.
Extract from 'Student stands by Tammy Wynette for geography degree' by Paul Stokes copyright © The Telegraph 2002, first published in *The Daily Telegraph* 19.07.02, reprinted by permission of the publisher.
Extract from 'How the opera is being repackaged to appeal to young school children' by Tim Walker copyright © The Independent 2007, first published in *The Independent* 22.03.07, reprinted by permission of the publisher.
Extract from 'Hippo Heaven' by Mark Debble copyright © BBC Wildlife 2003, first published in *BBC Wildlife* Magazine February 2003, reprinted by permission of the publisher.
Extract from *Rainforest Concern Advertisement: We Have a Choice* copyright © Rainforest Concern, reprinted by permission of the publisher.
Extract from *The World Without Us* by Alan Weisman (Virgin Books, 2007) copyright © Alan Weisman 2007, reprinted by permission of the publisher.
Extract from 'Give them stick' by John Litchfield copyright © The Independent 2004, first published in *The Independent* 24.03.04, reprinted by permission of the publisher.
Extract from 'Britain is the ready-meal glutton' by Anthony Browne copyright © N I Syndication 2003, first published in *The Times* 21.02.03, reprinted by permission of the publisher.
Extract from 'Elderly lose £40 million in distraction' by John Steele copyright © The Telegraph 2001, first published in *The Daily Telegraph* 28.12.01, reprinted by permission of the publisher.
Extract from 'What's so good about EMA?' from *www.direct.gov.uk*, copyright © HMSO.
Extract from 'Who needs money when you've got a spring in your step?' by Hermoione Eyre copyright © The Independent 2004, first published in *The Independent* 17.03.04, reprinted by permission of the publisher.
Extract from 'Giving money away makes you feel better – especially if you're a woman' by Steve Connor copyright © The Independent 2007, first published in *The Independent* 15.06.07, reprinted by permission of the publisher.
Extract from 'The joy of modern life' by Rachel Ragg copyright © The Independent 1999, first published in *The Independent* 21.12.99, reprinted by permission of the publisher.



The authors and publishers would like to thank the following for permission to reproduce their photographs:
**Alamy** pp20, 44
**Corbis** pp4,9, 58
Eye Ubiquitous pp36, 68, 92
Image Source pp13, 32, 72
**Jupite**r pp39, 84



Printed and bound in Thailand

2012 2011 2010 2009 2008
10 9 8 7 6 5 4 3 2 1

# Contents

# 1 Aiming high

## Reading

CAE Part 4

### Multiple matching

1 Read the article about the explorer Ranulph Fiennes quickly. In the article, is he mainly

**A** giving advice to inexperienced explorers?
**B** talking about the nature of exploration?
**C** promoting adventure travel to young people?

2 For questions **1–15**, answer by choosing from the sections of the article **(A–G)**. Some of the choices may be required more than once.

**In which section are the following mentioned?**

| | |
|---|---|
| the suggestion that Fiennes still seems enthusiastic about exploration | **1** ____ |
| an aspect of Fiennes's character that has been unfairly highlighted | **2** ____ |
| a negative effect of the growing interest in adventure travel | **3** ____ |
| a reason Fiennes gives for exploration becoming more appealing to amateurs | **4** ____ |
| a misconception regarding the knowledge previous explorers had | **5** ____ |
| Fiennes's fascination with a field in which he is fairly inexperienced | **6** ____ |
| Fiennes's opinion that someone who is reasonably fit could reach the South Pole | **7** ____ |
| the belief that explorers have too much respect for their own field | **8** ____ |
| the view that only professional explorers were capable of reaching distant destinations | **9** ____ |
| the instinctive human desire to explore new places | **10** ____ |
| the suggestion that more care is taken on difficult routes | **11** ____ |
| Fiennes's primary motivation for being an explorer | **12** ____ |
| the importance given by explorers to achieving something before anyone else | **13** ____ |
| Fiennes being held in high regard by other adventurers | **14** ____ |
| Fiennes's suggestion that people find increasingly unusual ways to achieve recognition | **15** ____ |

# Is this your idea of fun?

*Sir Ranulph Fiennes is the world's greatest living explorer. But now it seems an endless stream of people are conquering the South Pole or clambering up Everest. Mark MacKenzie asks him, is the exploring game becoming too easy?*

**A**
In the field of human exploration, Sir Ranulph Fiennes's personal achievements are remarkable and his numerous expeditions to the North and South Poles have turned him into an iconic figure, the explorer's explorer. Now there are many amateurs that would follow in his footsteps. Adventure travel is one of the fastest growing sectors of the travel market. Offering trips to destinations including Mount Everest, Antarctica and the South Pole, tour companies can now provide access for those less tough to remote parts of the planet once considered the exclusive playgrounds of Fiennes and his peers.

**B**
This year, record numbers are expected at the base camp of Everest, in the hope of reaching the summit of the world's tallest peak. So, is the exploring game getting too easy? 'Anyone who plans carefully could get to the South Pole if they're in relatively good condition and go at the right time of year,' says Fiennes. 'I would say the same of Mount Everest. If the weather's good and you take a reasonable guide, you should be able to get up even if you've never climbed before. However, there are still plenty of expeditions the majority of the public would not be able to do. Crossing the whole continent of Antarctica unsupported, for example, your troubles only really start at the South Pole. But the urge to go to far-flung regions is innate to man,' Fiennes continues, 'and I think provided there is no ecological damage, this is fine. On Everest, though, there has been a dramatic impact in terms of litter.'

**C**
But with specialist companies willing to deposit increasing numbers of tourists in ever more remote locations, is exploring still a true test of character? 'The challenge is what you make of it,' says Fiennes. 'In the wrong weather, you can have the most horrendous time on reasonably easy routes. But the ratio of accidents on Everest or at the South Pole is less than that on certain tourist routes, because you expect to be very cold and encounter crevasses and so you are naturally more cautious.' Also lying behind the increasing numbers of extreme adventurers, says Fiennes, is the improved technology used for polar equipment. 'It's all a lot lighter now, less bulky. If you're inexperienced, that makes these journeys a lot more appealing.'

**D**
Patrick Woodhead, whose young team reached the South Pole in 75 days, thinks the explorer community has a tendency to be overly reverential towards their discipline and claims his South Pole trek was a thoroughly enjoyable experience. However, last year, Fiennes published a biography of the original Antarctic explorer, Captain Robert Falcon Scott, and he feels there are those among modern explorers who remain ignorant of the debt they owe to Scott's pioneering spirit. 'People today think we knew back then that Antarctica was a continent – we didn't. On his first expedition to Antarctica in 1902, Scott made an 800-mile journey when the furthest expedition previously had been 14 miles.'

**E**
What is it that has driven explorers to the extremes of the Earth? 'Explorers have always had a thousand different motives,' Fiennes acknowledges. 'If I'm asked myself, I am quite clear. It's my profession and how I make an income. There are people who aren't comfortable with that. I'm supposed to say "Because it's there to be conquered." I think some people still need this image of nobility.' Such frankness has contributed to Fiennes's reputation for occasional haughtiness. On an expedition in 1971, he made the mistake of taking along a television crew. 'It meant good publicity for future expeditions,' he says, 'but they deliberately set out with the aim of showing me up as a dictator.'

**F**
Nevertheless, Fiennes has built his reputation on the only sort of accomplishment that matters among his peers – being first. 'When Sir Edmund Hillary first scaled Everest, he used every aid at his disposal. The next "first" then has to be the person to do it without oxygen, then the first solo ascent and so on.' So are there any true 'firsts' left? 'In part, it's the attitude of the individual,' he says. 'If something has been done, they will find their own firsts. Eventually, expeditions end up relying on gimmicks; for example, going to the South Pole on a motorbike, or on a camel and so on.'

**G**
In 1992, Fiennes completed his first archaeological expedition to find the lost city of Ubar in the deserts of Oman. He admits he found the detective work intriguing, albeit a challenge for a relative amateur, and believes the possibility of making similar discoveries may increasingly occupy his time in the future. While most men his age are thinking about retirement, his appetite for adventure appears undiminished. Last November, he and Mike Stroud became the first men to run seven marathons in seven countries in as many days. Is adventuring getting too easy? Not just yet.

## Vocabulary

Wordlist on page 209 of the Coursebook.

### Verb and noun collocations

Complete each of the gaps with one of the words from the box.

| | | | | |
|---|---|---|---|---|
| out | with | in | to | into |

1 Their solar panel business **ran** ______ **problems** after a succession of wet summers in the mid-1990s.

2 Last year's police campaign to reduce the number of accidents on motorways **met** ______ **limited success**.

3 Union leaders have not **ruled** ______ **the possibility of** taking strike action.

4 Her attempt to cycle across the Sahara **ended** ______ **failure** yesterday, when she fell off her bike and broke her leg.

5 Taking on the Cup holders was no easy task, but they **rose** ______ **the challenge** and drew 1–1.

### Adjective and noun collocations

1 One of the items of vocabulary in each group is not normally used with the word in capitals. Cross out the item which does not fit. There is an example at the beginning **(0)**.

| | | | | | |
|---|---|---|---|---|---|
| **0** | distinct | ~~heavy~~ | remote | strong | **POSSIBILITY** |
| **1** | fair | inside | realistic | slim | **CHANCE** |
| **2** | potential | recurrent | resounding | trivial | **PROBLEM** |
| **3** | burning | daunting | exciting | fresh | **CHALLENGE** |
| **4** | hard | high | personal | poor | **MOTIVATION** |
| **5** | huge | overnight | roaring | terrible | **SUCCESS** |
| **6** | continued | dismal | inevitable | urgent | **FAILURE** |
| **7** | heated | lifelong | greatest | secret | **AMBITION** |
| **8** | major | outlying | remarkable | sporting | **ACHIEVEMENT** |

2 Complete each space with an appropriate adjective from exercise 1. There is an example at the beginning **(0)**.

**0** I can't understand why he applied for the job; there was**n't even a** *remote* **possibility** that he'd get it.

**1** Recent corruption scandals mean that the party now stands **only a** ________ **chance of** victory in the forthcoming elections.

**2** During his adolescence, serious illness was a ________ **problem**, and always seemed to strike at exam time.

**3** The situation does pose **a rather** ________ **challenge**, but we will not be put off.

**4** His consistently low marks seem to be both the result and the cause of ________ **motivation**.

**5** The book brought her great wealth and worldwide fame, but this was **no** ________ **success**; her previous two novels had been bestsellers in her own country.

**6** It was a night of ________ **failure** for British athletes, whose recent successes had given cause for great optimism.

**7** As I've always said, it's been a ________ **ambition** of mine to play Hamlet, and now at last I can fulfil it.

**8** Undoubtedly, the greatest ________ **achievement** of the year was Alek Schmidt's record-breaking marathon run of two hours and four minutes.

## Word formation

Complete each gap with an appropriate noun form of the word in capitals at the end of the sentence. There is an example at the beginning **(0)**.

**Don't forget!**

You may need to use the negative or plural form of the noun.

**0** Many people at the club are questioning the *wisdom* of signing the 16-year-old goalkeeper. **WISE**

**1** Excessive __________ to direct sunlight should of course be avoided. **EXPOSE**

**2** Councillors have once again rejected __________ for a new multi-storey car park. **PROPOSE**

**3** Management criticized the unions for their stubborn attitude and __________ in the wage negotiations. **FLEXIBLE**

**4** The government is concerned at the number of unfilled __________ in the nursing profession. **VACANT**

**5** There is a strong feeling within the company that greater __________ should be placed on staff development. **EMPHASIZE**

**6** Failure to meet legal safety __________ has led to the temporary closure of the fairground. **REQUIRE**

**7** She chose to live in Brighton because of its mild climate and __________ to London. **CLOSE**

**8** There is a chronic __________ of housing in our cities. **SHORT**

**9** The complete __________ of this answer shows that the candidate did not read the question carefully. **RELEVANT**

**10** He achieved __________ for failing a drugs test after winning an Olympic final. **NOTORIOUS**

# Language focus

Grammar reference on page 216 of the Coursebook.

## Spelling

The following letter contains **20** spelling mistakes. Find the mistakes and correct them.

*Dear Sir,*

*I am writting to complain about an article that apeared in the 'Winners and Loosers' section in last weekend's edition of your newspaper.*

*The article, wich analyses the growth of my educational publishing company, 'ABC', describes me as 'a man with surprisingly little education' and attributes my success to 'agresive ambition and a complete disregard for the wellfare of his employees'. This is, of course, totaly untrue, and although I do not intend to justify myself or my business methods, their are one or two observations I feel I ougth to make.*

*Firstly, the economics degree I obtained from Bristol University speaks for itself, particularly, I feel, as I graduated with first class honours. In adition, whilst I am proud to consider myself ambitious, this is not at the expense of my staff, who would, I know, be only too pleased for you to intervue them. Indeed, they would be disappointed if they where not given the oportunity to inform your readers of their generous salary, impresive working conditions and excellent promotion prospects.*

*As you can imagine, your article has caused considerable pane and embarrassment, both too myself and my family, who found it extremly upsetting. I trust you will print an apology in the next edition of your newspaper, pointing out and rectifying the innacuracies in the article.*

*Yours faithfuly*

*John Austin*

## Modal verbs: *might, could, may, can*

1 In **1–7**, complete the second sentence so that it has the same meaning as the first. There is an example at the beginning **(0)**.

**0** Would you mind lending me your pen for a moment?
May *I borrow your pen for a moment* ?

**1** Although he lives here, we never see him.
He may ______________________________ .

**2** They're very likely to ask you to speak French during the interview.
You may ______________________________ .

**3** Perhaps she didn't know you were married.
She might ______________________________ .

**4** He had a good chance of getting the job, but he didn't apply.
If he'd applied for the job, he could ______________________________ .

**5** I rarely use my bike these days, so it would make sense if I sold it.
I rarely use my bike these days, so I may ______________________________ .

**6** Why on earth didn't you tell me you were vegetarian?
You might ______________________________ !

**7** It's unlikely she was enjoying herself very much.
She can't ______________________________ .

I rarely use my bike these days, so it would make sense if I sold it!

2 In **1–7**, one of the three alternatives is incorrect. Cross it out. There is an example at the beginning **(0)**.

**0** You ~~*might not*~~*/may not/cannot* leave until I give you permission.

**1** It's not my scarf – I think it *might/could/can* be Graham's.

**2** It *might/may/could* not be warm enough to eat outside tonight, but we'll keep our fingers crossed.

**3** He's so lazy – he *might/may/could* at least offer to do the washing up!

**4** I know you didn't want to come, but you *might/may/could* as well try and enjoy yourself now that you're here.

**5** Don't run across the road like that again – you *might/may/could* have been run over!

**6** It was a tough walk, but we *could/were able to/managed to* reach the end before it got dark.

**7** Police are now saying that the fire *might/may/could* not have been started deliberately, although they have refused to rule out the possibility of arson entirely.

## Use of English

CAE Part 1

### Multiple-choice cloze

For questions **1–12**, read the text below and then decide which answer **(A**, **B**, **C** or **D)** best fits each gap. There is an example at the beginning **(0)**.

### On top of the world

In May 1998, just two years after breaking his back in a parachuting accident whilst **(0)** ___ in the army, Bear Grylls became the youngest Briton to **(1)** ___ the summit of Mount Everest and return **(2)** ___ . He was just 23 years old.

As his back recovered and he regained his **(3)** ___ , Bear decided to leave the army in order to pursue his lifelong ambition to conquer the highest **(4)** ___ in the world. A friend of his was organising an expedition to Everest and Bear asked to **(5)** ___ . After a year spent preparing for the climb and **(6)** ___ sponsorship money, he and his companions moved out to the Himalayas to **(7)** ___ up the challenge.

In **(8)** ___ Bear spent over 10 weeks on the mountain's south-east face. This **(9)** ___ a whole week at Camp Two simply waiting for the right conditions to make his attempt on the summit. When he finally made it to the top, he sat for 20 minutes, just gazing in wonder at the **(10)** ___ before him.

The hardest part was still to come though. Every year the number of climbers killed on Everest increases, with most deaths occurring on the descent. It is **(11)** ___ surprising then, that Bear should feel a **(12)** ___ sense of relief when he eventually got back to base camp. Three British climbers under 25 have tried to conquer Everest; Bear is the only one to survive.

| | | | |
|---|---|---|---|
| **0 A** assisting | **B** obeying | **C** ordering | **D** <u>serving</u> |
| **1 A** achieve | **B** reach | **C** get | **D** attain |
| **2 A** live | **B** lively | **C** living | **D** alive |
| **3 A** power | **B** force | **C** vigour | **D** strength |
| **4 A** crest | **B** crown | **C** peak | **D** tip |
| **5 A** join | **B** unite | **C** attach | **D** link |
| **6 A** rising | **B** raising | **C** arising | **D** arousing |
| **7 A** take | **B** rise | **C** face | **D** put |
| **8 A** summary | **B** short | **C** total | **D** conclusion |
| **9 A** contained | **B** included | **C** comprised | **D** consisted |
| **10 A** eyesight | **B** outlook | **C** vision | **D** view |
| **11 A** strongly | **B** equally | **C** rarely | **D** hardly |
| **12 A** great | **B** large | **C** wide | **D** full |

# Writing

**CAE Part 2**

## Competition entries

1 Read the following Writing Part 2 task.

You see the following announcement in an international magazine:

> **Greatest sportsperson competition**
>
> We are planning a series of TV programmes about the 10 greatest sportsmen and women of all time. Which sportsperson would you nominate to be included in the series? Write to us describing this person's achievements and explaining why you feel he or she should be included.

Write your **competition entry in 220–260** words.

2 In the entry below, the name of the nominee has been covered with ink stains. Read the entry and decide which of the tennis players **A–D** is described.

**A** Ivan Lendl
**B** Ilie Năstase
**C** Björn Borg
**D** Boris Becker

*[redacted] was without doubt the most outstanding tennis player of his generation and one of the all-time sporting greats. In the late 1970s this highly talented young man put all other players in the shade and your forthcoming series would be incomplete without a programme about him.*

*It is the fact that he achieved so much so young that makes him such a strong candidate for a nomination. In 1974, at the age of seventeen, he became the youngest man to hold a Grand Slam singles title, the French Open, which he went on to win another five times in the next seven years. And as a twenty-year-old he became the youngest ever Wimbledon champion, a title he claimed five times in a row. Whether on grass or clay, he outclassed all the other big names of his era.*

*Admittedly, some of the records he set have since been equalled or broken, and he lost four US Open finals to Jimmy Connors and John McEnroe. But what set him apart from these players was his cool temperament, which helped him remain calm under pressure and earned him the nickname 'Ice Man'. And with his two-handed backhand and powerful shots from the baseline, he changed the face of tennis and had a strong influence on the way the game is played today.*

*[redacted] retired when he was just 26. Who knows what else he might have achieved if he'd continued playing, but the fact that he stopped at the height of his career helped make him into a legend and he surely deserves a place among your top ten greatest sportspeople.*

3 What is the purpose of the first and last paragraphs in the model?

4 In which part or parts of the model does the writer describe the nominee's achievements?

What reasons does the writer give for including him in the TV series?

5 Find examples of words and phrases in the model which express the fact that the nominee was a good sportsperson and/or better than others.

eg *the most outstanding tennis player of his generation*

6 Either:
**a** write your own answer to the task in exercise 1.
or:
**b** write an answer for one of the following competitions:

- The greatest writer of all time
- The greatest living actor/actress
- The most talented musician of the last thirty years
- The most influential political leader of all time

You should write **220–260** words.

Before you write your answer, read the **Don't forget box** and do the exercise in the **Useful language section** below.

## Don't forget!

- Plan your answer before you write.
- Address all the points in the task.
- Use a range of vocabulary.
- Write in a consistent register.
- Finish with a strong final paragraph.

## Useful language

Complete each of the expressions with a word from the box.

| | | | | | | | |
|---|---|---|---|---|---|---|---|
| ability | class | gift | head | match | none | peak | standard |

**1** As a jazz musician, Charlie Parker was **in a** _________ **of his own.**

**2** Iain M Banks **stands** _________ **and shoulders above** other science-fiction writers of his generation.

**3** When she was **at her** _________ she won 17 consecutive races on the international circuit.

**4** She is **unrivalled in her** _________ **to** portray downtrodden characters who struggle to overcome their difficulties.

**5** Borg was **more than a** _________ **for** Vilas and the Swede won in straight sets.

**6** Early on in his career he showed a _________ **for** writing short stories.

**7** As a football player Maradona was **second to** _________.

**8** Her acting is always **of the highest** _________.

# 2 Times change

## Reading

**CAE Part 3**

### Multiple choice

You are going to read a magazine article about the first people to arrive in the Americas. For questions **1–7**, choose the answer **(A**, **B**, **C** or **D)** which you think fits best according to the text.

# Island hopping to a new world

Digging in a dank limestone cave in Canada's Queen Charlotte Islands last summer, Christina Heaton hardly noticed the triangular piece of chipped stone she'd unearthed in a pile of debris. Then, as her scientist father, Timothy, sifted through the muck, he realized her unwitting find was actually invaluable. It was a spear point. Bear bones found near the artefact indicated its owner had presumably speared the beast, which later retreated into the cave and eventually died with the point still lodged in its loins. Radiocarbon tests soon dated the remains at about 12,000 years old, making them the earliest signs of human activity in the region or, for that matter, in all of the Americas.

Almost from the moment the first white explorers set eyes on America's indigenous 'Indians', people have wondered where they came from. Fray Jose Acosta, a Jesuit priest, was one of the first to make a sensible conjecture in 1590 that a small group from Asia's northernmost latitudes must have walked to the New World. Indeed, since the 1930s archaeologists have taught that the first Americans were hunters who crossed the Bering land bridge from Siberia, chasing mammoths southward through Canada down a narrow corridor between two ice sheets. By about 11,500 years ago, they'd got as far as Clovis, New Mexico, near where archaeologists first found their distinctive spear points. Their descendants ultimately reached the tip of South America after a footslogging journey begun more than 20,000 miles away. Or so the story goes.

Yet the Heatons' find is the latest addition to a small but weighty pile of tools and human remains suggesting the first Americans may have come from Asia not down the centre of the continent but along the coast in boats, centuries or millenniums prior to the Clovis people. The evidence that Heaton and his colleagues are seeking has turned up along the Pacific coast all the way from Alaska to southern Chile. So far it does not include any human remains of pre-Clovis age but a woman's bones were found on Santa Rosa Island off the Californian coast. While the bones show that the woman herself was alive 200–300 years after the Clovis people's long trek, it is likely that she was the descendant of earlier settlers. And scientists excavating Chile's Monte Verde site, over 6,000 miles from the southernmost Clovis find, have discovered medicinal herbs and artefacts that date back over 12,500 years.

Such finds have backed up genetic and biological research to paint a far more complex picture of America's first explorers. Rather than a single migration of Clovis people, 'there were clearly several waves of human exploration,' says Douglas Wallace, a geneticist at the University of California-Irvine. Wallace's DNA studies of American natives identify at least five genetically distinct waves, four from Asia and one possibly of early European descent, the earliest of which could have arrived more than 20,000 years ago. That diversity concurs with research by linguists who argue the Americas' 143 native languages couldn't have all developed from a single 11,500-year-old tongue. And if they had, then the languages would be the most diverse along the mainland route the Clovis people travelled. In fact, the number of languages is greatest along the Pacific coast, adding to suspicions that at least some of the first immigrants came that way.

Until recently, many geologists assumed that the Ice-Age shore was a glaciated wasteland. But new studies of fossils and ancient climates imply a navigable coastline full of shellfish and other foods, with grassy inland tundra capable of supporting large animals – and perhaps sea-faring humans heading south. Unfortunately, the evidence that could prove the coastal-migration scenario is well and truly hidden. Warming temperatures since the last Ice Age have transformed the ancient tundra into thick forests, rendering most signs of early human exploration all but invisible and melting Ice-Age glaciers have submerged most of the coastal campsites where the ancient mariners may have stayed a while.

In 1998, archaeologist Daryl Fedje retrieved an ancient hunting blade, one of the first human artefacts found in the region. This inspired some to call for a comprehensive high-tech search of the sea floor yet the immense costs of a seafloor survey have prevented this. So Fedje and other researchers have instead focused on caves on the nearby islands and in Alaska, where artefacts are protected from weather and decay. 'The caves have been a real windfall,' says Heaton of the animal bones he has found. He's confident that it's just a matter of time before he and his colleagues find pre-Clovis human remains because 'in almost every cave we put our shovels to, we find something new.'

## Don't forget!

The questions follow the same order as the information in the text.

1 When Tim Heaton noticed the spear point, he was
  **A** certain that an important discovery had been made.
  **B** reluctant to speculate how it had arrived in the cave.
  **C** surprised to find such an artefact located in that area.
  **D** disappointed that it was not something more significant.

2 What are we told about archaeologists in the 1930s?
  **A** They agreed with Jose Acosta's theory about the route taken by the first migrants to North America.
  **B** They believed that the weapons had become more sophisticated by the time migrants had reached New Mexico.
  **C** They theorized that the earliest group of migrants remained in Canada.
  **D** They were unaware of the distance that early hunters had really travelled.

3 The writer uses the phrase 'Or so the story goes' (line 30) to
  **A** question the accuracy of the actual distance that migrants travelled.
  **B** illustrate how human ambition can lead to remarkable achievement.
  **C** point out the significance of preserving historical records.
  **D** suggest that traditional archaeological theory may be wrong.

4 What point is exemplified by the references to the find on Santa Rosa Island?
  **A** The Clovis people could have had the ability to build primitive boats.
  **B** The Clovis people were the earliest of the migrant groups to explore the coast.
  **C** The Clovis people may have been on the mainland after other migrants were on the island.
  **D** The Clovis people's descendants must have spread out in search of new territory.

5 The research that Douglas Wallace has carried out
  **A** shows early migrants were more sophisticated than previously thought.
  **B** indicates that the first settlers in America were most likely from Europe.
  **C** suggests that the Clovis people had reached America over 20,000 years ago.
  **D** supports the argument proposed by linguists about native American languages.

6 What does the writer state about the possible route that early migrants took?
  **A** The Ice-Age had little significant impact on the American coastline.
  **B** It is virtually impossible to find proof of migration on this route.
  **C** The early travellers probably chose this route for its food supplies.
  **D** Certain archaeologists are looking for a route that never existed.

7 Timothy Heaton decided to excavate caves in the Queen Charlotte Islands because
  **A** a thorough exploration of the sea bed is not feasible.
  **B** his research team are in direct competition with Daryl Fedje's.
  **C** human remains have already been found in this location.
  **D** there may another layer of artefacts under the Clovis layer.

# Vocabulary

Wordlist on page 210 of the Coursebook.

## Changes

1 For questions **1–4**, complete each of the gaps with a word from the box. The verb you choose must be appropriate for the gaps in both sentences. There is an example at the beginning **(0)**.

| |
|---|
| adapted |
| altered |
| shifted |
| transferred |

**0 a** I've *changed* **my mind** – I'll have the soup instead of the prawn cocktail.
**b** He *changed* **places with** Jean so that he could sit nearer the blackboard.

**1 a** Football star David Beckham was ___________ from Manchester United to Real Madrid **for a fee of** £25 million.
**b** I've just ___________ £3,000 from my current account to my savings account.

**2 a** When asked why he hadn't done his homework, James ___________ **uncomfortably in his seat**.
**b** The publishing company has ___________ **its attention away from** children's literature **towards** school text books.

**3 a** The snow leopard has ___________ **to life** at altitudes of up to 6,000 metres.
**b** Several of her **books** have been ___________ **for television**.

**4 a** The jacket was a perfect fit, but I **had the trousers** ___________ because they were a little too tight.
**b** The new tower block has dramatically ___________ **the appearance** of the town.

2 Underline the word **A**, **B**, **C** or **D** which best fits each space.

**1** He's _____ changed at all since I last saw him – just as lively and outgoing as he always was.
**A** slightly **B** hardly **C** subtly **D** nearly

**2** The seat is _____ adjusted by pulling on this lever here.
**A** highly **B** fully **C** openly **D** easily

**3** Prices vary _____ , so do shop around before you buy your barbecue.
**A** widely **B** instantly **C** completely **D** closely

**4** In response to growing criticism, the government modified its plans for education cuts, though only very _____ .
**A** barely **B** fundamentally **C** slightly **D** faintly

**5** To her credit, she _____ transformed the business from a string of small shops into a major international chain of department stores.
**A** radically **B** revoltingly **C** enormously **D** increasingly

3 Complete each of the gaps with one of the words from the box.

| |
|---|
| fortunes |
| heart |
| scene |
| pace |
| condition |
| attitudes |
| direction |
| law |

**1** You should go away somewhere for the weekend. **A change of** ___________ will do you good.

**2** At first my parents refused to let me go off travelling on my own, but then they **had a change of** ___________ .

**3** After a very slow start, the car chase gives the film **a** much needed **change of** ___________ .

**4** In **a complete change of** ___________ he gave up his job in teaching and became a farmer.

**5** The win **marked a change in the** ___________ of the team, which had lost its previous six games.

**6** Despite the operation on his eye, there has been **no significant change in the patient's** ___________ .

**7** For many years, anti-smoking campaigners had **called for a change in the** ___________ to make it illegal for people to smoke in bars and cafés.

**8** The legalization of divorce reflected **a change in** ___________ **towards** marriage.

**Self-help**

Add the expressions in bold in exercise 3 to your vocabulary notebook.

## Language focus

Grammar reference on page 216 of the Coursebook.

1 Correct the following sentences by changing the underlined word or words. You may need to write more than one word. There is an example at the beginning **(0)**.

*have known*
**0** I <u>know</u> him since we were at school together.

**1** We <u>would</u> have a parrot, but he flew away one day when I was cleaning his cage.
**2** The service was terrible; when our dessert arrived, Paul still <u>ate</u> his starter!
**3** I <u>have met</u> some very interesting people on my holiday last year.
**4** This must be about the tenth time I <u>eat</u> in this restaurant.
**5** It's a long time since we <u>don't see</u> each other.
**6** It wasn't the first time she <u>was catching</u> him taking money from her purse.
**7** I'd like to <u>stay</u> in London longer, but we had to get back for Sandra's wedding.
**8** I'd rather you <u>didn't give</u> him my phone number – he phoned me three times yesterday!
**9** You <u>did</u> nothing but complain since we've been here.
**10** She was about <u>sitting</u> down, when she noticed the chair was broken.

2 Complete each of the gaps with an appropriate tense or form of the verb in brackets.

**A**

Derek Taylor, 87, is one of Britain's longest-serving Santas: he **(1)** ___________ (put) on his red suit and white beard for nearly 50 years now. He believes he **(2)** ___________ (manage) to hold down his job in a Rotherham department store for so long by adapting to the changing attitudes of the children he **(3)** ___________ (meet) down the years. 'Back in the 1950s, children **(4)** ___________ (believe) in Father Christmas totally and **(5)** ___________ (ask) lots of questions, like "Where exactly do you live?" or "How do you manage to squeeze down chimneys?" Nowadays they just tell me about the presents they want. Of course, the toys they ask for **(6)** ___________ (change) dramatically over the years. In the old days, if you **(7)** ___________ (say) you would try and bring them the doll or roller skates they wanted, their faces **(8)** ___________ (light) up. Now it's all mobile phones, computers and DVD players.'

**B**

I'll never forget the time I **(1)** ___________ (go) to the hairdresser's in the early 1950s for my first perm, or 'permanent wave', after I **(2)** ___________ (see) a picture of Gina Lollobrigida with one in a film magazine. I **(3)** ___________ (work) in a shop at the time, and I **(4)** ___________ (book) an appointment for 1.30 pm on Wednesday afternoon, my half day off. **(5)** ___________ (wash) and cut my hair, the hairdresser rolled it into tight and rather painful metal curlers. He then connected the curlers to wires from a machine that looked as if it **(6)** ___________ (just/land) from outer space! He chose that moment to tell me he **(7)** ___________ (experience) problems with the machine for the last few days and that the 'baking' procedure **(8)** ___________ (take) a little longer than expected. In fact, I **(9)** ___________ (spend) over six hours in the hairdresser's altogether and **(10)** ___________ (not/arrive) home until well after 8 o'clock! At one point during my long ordeal, after I **(11)** ___________ (sit) in the same chair for about four hours, my worried husband phoned the hairdresser's to ask what time I **(12)** ___________ (leave). It was the first time I **(13)** ___________ (ever/have) a perm, and I decided there and then that it **(14)** ___________ (be) my last!

# Use of English

CAE Part 3

## Word formation

For questions **1–10**, use the word given in capitals at the end of some of the lines to form a word that fits in the gap **in the same line**. There is an example at the beginning **(0)**.

### Book review: *Walls have Ears* by Mark Mitchell

| | |
|---|---|
| Avid **(0)** _readers_ of Mark Mitchell's critically acclaimed historical novels will not | **READ** |
| be disappointed by his **(1)** ________ offering, *Walls have Ears*, a simple, but | **LATE** |
| **(2)** ________ written tale of childhood innocence in a world of adult corruption. | **BEAUTY** |
| Mitchell, a former history teacher, shot to fame three years ago thanks to the television | |
| **(3)** ________ of his fourth novel, *Baroque of Ages*, which followed the fortunes of | **ADAPT** |
| two teenage siblings in seventeenth-century Britain. Despite the author's **(4)** ________ | **SATISFY** |
| with the TV production, **(5)** ________ Marian Blackshaw and Edek Sobera, it was a | **STAR** |
| huge success and **(6)** ________ of his books for children rocketed overnight as a | **SELL** |
| result. *Walls have Ears* is a **(7)** ________ on the central theme of *Baroque of Ages*, | **VARY** |
| though this time set against the background of Hadrian's Wall during its construction in | |
| the second century. The chance **(8)** ________ by two young friends of a plot to | **DISCOVER** |
| assassinate the Roman Emperor responsible for the defensive wall turns their world | |
| upside down. The children are sworn to secrecy, but their conscience **(9)** ________ | **THREAT** |
| to get the better of them. **(10)** ________ have criticized Mitchell for being too | **HISTORY** |
| liberal with the facts, but this will not deter his young fans from queueing up for their | |
| copy of the book when it is released on June 20th. | |

CAE Part 4

## Gapped sentences

For questions **1–5** below, think of **one** word only which can be used appropriately in all three sentences. In this exercise, the words required can be found on page 27 of the Coursebook. Here is an example **(0)**.

**0** There has been a recent _shift_ **towards** domestic tourism with fewer people booking overseas holidays.

The government plans to _shift_ **its attention away** from punishing crime to crime prevention.

I'm changing to a different _shift_ next week so I'll be starting work much later.

**1** The aim of the campaign is to ________ **an end to** poverty in our inner cities.

The purpose of using old films in the classroom is to ________ **history alive** for the students.

The new water pump will ________ **about a** significant **change** in the lives of the local villagers.

**2** There were scratches along both ________ of my car when Julia returned it to me.

My mother always ________ **with** my brother whenever we have an argument.

The coach asked Ernesto to **change** ________ so both groups had an equal number of good players.

3 The ________ **of the painting** is thought to be the artist's mother.

The festival organizers would like to point out that all times and dates of events **are ________ to change**.

Some politicians **change the** __________ rather than answer a question they find awkward.

4 It's dangerous to __________ **lanes** on the motorway without indicating first.

Although **we flicked the**__________ a number of times, the machine would not work.

We will no longer be using the old accounting software after we _________ **over** to the new software next month.

5 I came home to find my son __________ **up** bits of glass from the kitchen floor.

The holiday brochure showed majestic forests __________ **over** the mountains.

The new boss has promised there will be __________ **changes** within our department.

CAE Part 5

## Key word transformations

For questions **1–8**, complete the second sentence so that it has a similar meaning to the first sentence, using the word given. **Do not change the word given**. You must use between **three** and **six** words, including the word given. Here is an example **(0)**.

**0** I haven't driven an automatic car for several years.

**LAST**

It's *several years since I last drove* an automatic car.

**1** This is your third warning from me this week about being late for work.

**NOT**

This is the third time this week I ____________________ be late for work.

**2** I think Anita must have gone on a diet recently because she's quite slim now.

**HAS**

It looks as ____________________ dieting because she's quite slim now.

**3** I always hated pasta when I was a child but now I cook it regularly.

**USE**

I ____________________ pasta when I was a child but now I cook it regularly.

**4** I went to have my own look at the apartment and I couldn't understand why my friend wanted us to live in such a depressing place!

**SEE**

Having ____________________ myself, I couldn't understand why my friend wanted us to live in such a depressing place!

**5** We wanted to continue our mountain trek but the weather was too bad.

**LIKE**

We ____________________ on with our mountain trek but the weather was too bad.

**6** I want to inform you that I was not satisfied with the standard of service in your hotel.

**EXPRESS**

I would ____________________ with the standard of service in your hotel.

**7** I wanted to stay in last night but my flatmate insisted we go out.

**SOONER**

I ____________________ in last night but my flatmate insisted we go out.

**8** Didn't you want me to tell the staff about your resignation?

**RATHER**

Would ____________________ the staff know about your resignation?

# Writing

CAE Part 1

## Formal and informal letters

1 Read the following two Writing Part 1 tasks.

**A** You have just been on a week's historical tour of Rome. Your friend has written to you asking about your holiday. Read the magazine advertisement, the notes you have made, and the extract from your friend's letter and write a **letter** to your friend explaining which aspects were not satisfactory and giving her advice on how to prepare for her holiday.

**B** You have just been on a week's historical tour of Rome. Certain aspects of the tour have prompted you to write to the travel agency. Read the magazine advertisement and the notes you have made, and write a **letter** to Timson's Tours, explaining which aspects were not satisfactory and making recommendations for improvements.

### Timson's *Historical Tours*

**Seven days in Rome**

- Includes guided visits to the Pantheon, the Colosseum, the Sistine Chapel and a coach trip to the ancient Roman port of Ostia.
- There will also be two free days for you to do your own exploring with the help of our excellent guidebook, provided free of charge.
- Cost: £1,600, including return flights, four-star accommodation with bed and breakfast and coach trips in and around Rome.

*fantastic guide!* (guided visits)

*didn't get there – coach broke down* (Ostia)

*three – guide sick on last day* (two free days)

*no it isn't* (excellent)

*but not cost of admission to monuments!* (coach trips in and around Rome)

and I'm off to Rome with Timson's Tours next month. I'd be really interested to hear how you got on. Did it all go smoothly? Did you eat well?

I haven't been abroad for ages and I'd like to go as prepared as possible. Is there anything I should know before I go?

*yes, but restaurants very pricey* (eat well)

2 **A** and **B** below are the first half of the two letters required by the tasks. Use the underlined information in **A**, the informal letter, to complete the gaps in **B**, the formal letter. Write **one word** in each gap. There is an example at the beginning **(0)**.

**A**

Dear Sarah

Just got back from Rome and found your letter waiting for me. I had a very good week there – the guide, Francesca, really made it for me and I learnt loads about the history of Rome. She really knew her subject and she explained things so well.

So all in all I really enjoyed the holiday, but I've just written to Timson's to tell them about two or three things that happened when I was there. It's really a way of helping them to make things better for future tours – like the one you're going on next month!

For one thing, we never made it to Ostia because the coach broke down shortly after we left and the local rep didn't send another one to replace it. Also, we had three free days rather than two, because our guide suddenly fell ill at the end and we were left to look after ourselves. One last thing that'll be of particular interest to you – I only found out when I got to Rome that we had to pay to get into all the ancient monuments ourselves, which I thought was a bit cheeky considering the price.

That last point is certainly something for you to bear in mind when you go – make sure you ...

**B**

Dear Sir or Madam

I have just **(0)** *returned* from Rome, where I spent a week on one of your historical tours. I would like to express my general **(1)** ________________ with the holiday, during which I learnt a great **(2)** ________________ about Rome and its history. This was largely due to the excellent work of the guide, Francesca, who impressed everyone with her **(3)** ________________ and the quality of her **(4)** ________________.

I feel I should, however, draw your **(5)** ________________ to a number of incidents which occurred, in the hope that this may help you to **(6)** ________________ your service in future. **(7)** ________________, our planned visit to Ostia was cancelled, as the bus broke down soon after our **(8)** ________________ and your local representative **(9)** ________________ to send a replacement. In **(10)** ________________, our two free days became three, owing to the unexpected **(11)** ________________ of our guide on the final day; once again, we were not provided with a substitute. **(12)** ________________, I was rather surprised to **(13)** ________________ on my **(14)** ________________ in Rome that **(15)** ________________ fees to ancient monuments were not included in the price of the holiday.

As a result of my experience, I would like to make a number of recommendations for future tours.

**3** Now complete each of the letters, using the following plans as a guide. You should write **100–125 words for each letter.**

**A Giving advice to your friend**

*costs of admission – take enough money*

*guidebook poor – buy your own*

*restaurants can be pricey – check in guidebook/ask guide about cheap ones*

**B Making recommendations to Timson's**

*arrange alternative if bus breaks down, guide sick etc*

*make ad more explicit, eg admission costs*

*improve guidebook (say how)*

## Don't forget!

- Continue each letter using the same informal or formal register.
- End each letter in an appropriate way.
- Use a wide range of language.

## What to expect in the exam

In Part 1 you will be expected to write only one task type of 180–220 words.

# 3 Gathering information

## Reading

CAE Part 2

### Gapped text

You are going to read an extract from a magazine article. Six paragraphs have been removed from the extract. Choose from the paragraphs **A–G** the one that fits each gap **(1–6)**. There is one extra paragraph which you do not need to use.

**Don't forget!**

Read through the whole of the base text (the main text with the gaps) before you start to make your choices.

# The house of maps

**The world of geography owes a big debt to Stanfords, suppliers of maps to the world for over 150 years. Peter Whitfield traces the company's early history.**

During the winter of 1887, art critic John Ruskin wrote to a well-known London shop for help: *Gentlemen, have you any school atlas on sale at present without railroads in its maps? Of all the entirely odd stupidities of modern education, railroads in maps are infinitely the oddest to my mind.* The recipient of this rather strange appeal was the firm of Edward Stanford, the map-seller who had made himself pre-eminent in his field.

1 ______

The first Edward Stanford launched his business in 1853 when he took over the map shop of Trelawney Saunders in Charing Cross, London. He had left school at 14 to learn printing, moving on to work in a number of shops before joining Saunders in the map trade. Of course there were trade rivals but what put them ahead was Stanford's recognition that the 19th century was experiencing a rising demand for maps of all kinds.

2 ______

Of the personality of the first Edward Stanford we know little, but his son, the second Edward Stanford who became head of the firm in 1882, emerges more clearly, thanks to the survival of both business and personal papers. In his business letters he made it clear that *Stanfords* was no mere shop, but a service for gentlemen governed by gentlemen. His correspondents included some of the outstanding geographers of the age, many of whom commissioned *Stanfords* to make maps for them.

3 ______

It was under the second Stanford's direction that the firm's publishing programme reached its high-point with *Stanford's London Atlas of Universal Geography*, first issued in 1887, containing almost 100 detailed maps. As a textual companion to the atlas, the firm also published the magnificent *Stanford's Compendium of Geography and Travel*, a six-volume encyclopaedia of geography written by a team of first-class scholars.

4 ______

This could only be of benefit to sales and the rewards were substantial. Stanford prospered, the business was entirely his own and he spent its profits freely. He sent his three sons to Oxford University, bought a large villa in a London suburb and invested in the stock exchange. This prosperity was a world away from the lowly tradesman's upbringing his father had known in the 1830s. A reversal of fortune, however, was soon to come.

5

He would have been relieved to know that all three sons survived and that Edward Fraser Stanford returned from the Middle East to become director of the business. But a historical and social chasm had opened up between the pre-war world and the 1920s. The family's earlier prosperity, a university education and the army had transformed the mental horizons of the Stanford children: they lost their enthusiasm for trade and preferred their lives as officers and gentlemen.

6

This freed *Stanfords* to concentrate on retailing and, finally, to take advantage of the revolution in travel that began to gather pace in the late 1960s. The package tourist heading for the beaches has little use for maps, but for the independent traveller, maps are essential companions. By importing maps from the four corners of the globe, *Stanfords* has maintained its unique role as a leader in mapping and travel literature, even though this material is no longer published by *Stanfords* itself.

A Local governors, railway or mining engineers, newspaper editors and tourists all increasingly required maps, and within a few short years of his appointment at the shop, Stanford had initiated a map-publishing programme that would become the most comprehensive in England. After securing the rights to sell official maps produced by overseas and colonial survey authorities, he set about reducing this detailed survey information into smaller-scale accurate and up-to-date maps.

B In contrast to his dealings with these figures, there were the day-to-day arguments with resentful trade rivals and tedious officials, not to mention insolent customers. On more than one occasion Stanford hears himself verbally abused when he asks for overdue payments.

C Alongside these achievements, the Stanford name was synonymous with the maps of Ordnance Survey but they also acted as sales agent for many other official bodies, including *The Royal Geographical Society* and the War Office. Its role as distributor of these official survey maps gave the business a unique status, reinforcing the perception that its own maps must be authoritative and accurate.

D Consequently, some vital energy seemed to desert the business: the golden age of *Stanfords*' map-publishing was over, and the firm was ill-equipped to survive the years of economic depression ahead. The struggling business was eventually sold to George Philip and all *Stanfords*' map-making activities were absorbed into those of the parent company.

E Whether you sought an Ordnance Survey map of an English county or the goldfields of South Africa, such a reputation meant that *Stanfords* was always the first port of call. Over 150 years later, Stanfords continues to flourish as a map-seller, and is still renowned for its small but intriguing role in Britain's political and social history.

F The First World War was to all but eliminate the firm. Many of its staff became soldiers; private foreign travel virtually halted overnight; and all three of Stanford's sons were commissioned as junior officers. The effect was catastrophic and the strain on the ageing 'governor' proved fatal: when he died the firm was deep in debt and its future looked dark.

G This was a risk that Stanford was willing to take. Their property was rebuilt and reopened at Covent Garden with a splendid new showroom and space for all the cartographical and printing work on the floors above.

## Vocabulary

Wordlist on page 210 of the Coursebook.

### Adjective and noun collocations

1 Complete the crossword using the clues below. Each of the answers is a noun which collocates with the adjective in bold. All the collocations have appeared in units **1–3** of the Coursebook.

**Across**

**3** He hopes to fulfil his **burning** ________ to become world champion.

**5** The kitchen was filled with the **mouth-watering** ________ of freshly baked bread.

**6** Mailshots have proved to be the most **cost effective** ________ of marketing our products.

**8** The organizers claim that the demonstration was 'a **resounding** ________'.

**11** It made a **welcome** ________ to win – I was getting tired of losing.

**12** She now faces the **daunting** ________ of writing a successful sequel to her hugely popular first book.

**Down**

**1** The Prime Minister yesterday announced **sweeping** ________ to her Cabinet.
**2** He could smell the **acrid** ________ of rotten eggs.
**4** The newspaper has been accused of publishing **misleading** ________ in relation to the case.
**7** The government claims that the demonstration was 'a **dismal** ________'.
**9** We still have an **outside** ________ of qualifying for the finals.
**10** The pile of old clothes gave off a damp, **musty** ________ .

2 For each noun you wrote in exercise 1, write two further adjectives which collocate with it.

### Verb and noun collocations

1 Match each of the nouns in the box to one of the groups of verbs **1–8**. All the verbs in the group must collocate with the noun. The first one has been done for you.

| | | | |
|---|---|---|---|
| information | change | a problem | a possibility |
| a challenge | ~~success~~ | an ambition | a smell |

| | | | | |
|---|---|---|---|---|
| **1** achieve | deserve | enjoy | meet with | success |
| **2** achieve | fulfil | pursue | realize | ________ |
| **3** broadcast | gather | provide | publish | ________ |
| **4** face | present | rise to | take up | ________ |
| **5** bring about | call for | cope with | resist | ________ |
| **6** come up against | face up to | resolve | run into | ________ |
| **7** ignore | look into | overlook | rule out | ________ |
| **8** detect | get rid of | give off | leave | ________ |

2 Complete each of the gaps with the appropriate form of a verb from exercise 1. The first one has been done for you.

**1** He was a brilliant musician, who thoroughly _deserved_ the **success** he had – though I don't think it made him any happier.

**2** She still finds time to __________ her **ambition** to become a professional opera singer, though she is aware she may never achieve it.

**3** I've been __________ **information** on minority languages for my next book.

**4** The recent dramatic increase in the number of burglaries __________ a major **challenge** to the police.

**5** The only way to progress is by welcoming **change**, not __________ it.

**6** The company faced a number of **problems**, most of which it has now tackled and successfully __________ .

**7** We're currently __________ the **possibility** of opening new premises; it depends on the company's performance over the next year.

**8** It stinks of smoke in here! Could you open the window to __________ the **smell**?

## Word formation

Complete each gap with an appropriate form of the word in capitals at the end of the sentence. There is an example at the beginning **(0)**.

### Don't forget!

You may need to use the negative form of an adjective or adverb.

**0** As a student, I'm still _financially_ dependent on my parents. **FINANCE**

**1** Unfortunately, many people are still worryingly __________ of the facts about AIDS. **IGNORE**

**2** There are __________ versions of Vivaldi's *Four Seasons*, but this recording is by far the best I've heard. **COUNT**

**3** We'll have to walk to the village – it's __________ to cars. **ACCESS**

**4** We have discussed these problems on __________ occasions and still nothing has been decided. **NUMBER**

**5** Not __________ perhaps, sales of air conditioning systems increased considerably during the recent hot spell. **SURPRISE**

**6** *Bed of Roses*, widely seen as the finest __________ work about the period, was published in 1976. **LITERATE**

**7** After several __________ attempts, he finally passed his driving test in June last year. **SUCCEED**

**8** A __________ study of farming procedures in fifteen African countries has just been published. **COMPARE**

**9** Unemployment rose __________ last year. **DRAMA**

**10** As a special __________ offer, there is a 10% discount on all kitchen units in the new range. **INTRODUCE**

## Language focus

Grammar reference on page 217 of the Coursebook.

1 Complete each of the gaps with **two** words. Contractions (eg *haven't, don't* etc) count as two words. There is an example at the beginning **(0)**.

**0** She went on holiday with her friends, though we'd rather _she had_ come with us.

**1** It was a terrible film. I wish we __________ the French one instead.

**2** She found out from Jerry, but I'd __________ told her myself.

**3** If it hadn't __________ Eleanor's excellent negotiation skills, we might never have reached an agreement.

**4** I should __________ my gloves – my hands were freezing.

**5** Most employees would prefer __________ been given a bonus rather than an expensive Christmas hamper.

**6** __________ known he intended to resign, I'd never have sacked him.

**7** If only __________ spoken to me about it before; I __________ done something to help you.

**8** The accident __________ have happened if he hadn't __________ at 90 miles an hour.

2 Tick (✔) those endings which can complete the sentences. Either one, two or all three answers are possible.

**1** I'd much rather
**A** you have told me the truth.
**B** I have a motorbike than a car.
**C** have gone shopping on my own.

**2** If she didn't want to see you,
**A** she wouldn't have invited you to her party.
**B** what would you do?
**C** she used to get me to tell you she wasn't at home.

**3** If it hadn't been for the rain,
**A** we didn't get wet.
**B** we could have eaten outside.
**C** we've enjoyed ourselves very much.

**4** I couldn't have done it financially
**A** if my parents hadn't supported me.
**B** had it not been for the financial support of my parents.
**C** without the financial support of my parents.

**5** If you push that button,
**A** it goes faster.
**B** you'll regret it.
**C** nothing would happen.

**6** I wish I
**A** would have more time to do everything.
**B** had had more time to do everything.
**C** had more time to do everything.

**7** If I were to lend him the money,
**A** he hadn't paid it back.
**B** he wouldn't have paid it back.
**C** he'd have to pay it back soon.

**8** I'll tell her what you think
**A** if I happen to see her.
**B** should she be interested?
**C** if that's alright with you.

# Use of English

CAE Part 1

## Multiple-choice cloze

For questions **1–12**, read the text below and then decide which answer **(A**, **B**, **C** or **D)** best fits each gap. There is an example at the beginning **(0)**.

**Don't forget!**

Read the text through first before you start to make your choices.

### Garbology

To most people, landfill sites are **(0)** _____ holes in the ground where waste **(1)** _____ is buried. To garbologists, however, they provide a valuable **(2)** _____ of information about a population's activities in areas such as food consumption and waste disposal. Garbology is a branch of ethnography, a science which abandons traditional methods of **(3)** _____ market research information, such as questionnaires and focus groups, in favour of **(4)** _____ observation of people and their habits.

The world's **(5)** _____ garbologist, Professor William Rathje, is also an archaeologist. Archaeologists study past cultures by examining the **(6)** _____ of objects and buildings, but the basic principles of archaeology can also be applied to the discarded rubbish of present-day civilizations in order to **(7)** _____ a better understanding of how people behave now. As founder and director of the Garbage Project at the University of Arizona, Professor Rathje has **(8)** _____ over 30 years of his life to the archaeological study of modern refuse.

His work is of **(9)** _____ interest to commerce; companies need to understand the lives of their consumers in order to create brands which will be of most **(10)** _____ to them. Rathje's **(11)** _____ can help them achieve this. In addition, his analysis of the composition of landfill sites reveals a greater need not only to recycle more rubbish, but also to **(12)** _____ down on the amount of rubbish we produce in the first place.

| | | | |
|---|---|---|---|
| **0 A** easily | **B** <u>simply</u> | **C** bluntly | **D** directly |
| **1 A** selection | **B** product | **C** fabric | **D** material |
| **2 A** spring | **B** origin | **C** source | **D** fountain |
| **3 A** holding | **B** meeting | **C** obtaining | **D** comprising |
| **4 A** near | **B** close | **C** tight | **D** hard |
| **5 A** heading | **B** leading | **C** charging | **D** fronting |
| **6 A** rests | **B** ruins | **C** relics | **D** remains |
| **7 A** gain | **B** learn | **C** make | **D** gather |
| **8 A** conveyed | **B** devoted | **C** apportioned | **D** spent |
| **9 A** high | **B** large | **C** great | **D** deep |
| **10 A** function | **B** serving | **C** use | **D** purpose |
| **11 A** outcomes | **B** findings | **C** implications | **D** derivations |
| **12 A** lower | **B** cut | **C** bring | **D** get |

CAE Part 4

## Gapped sentences

For questions **1–5**, think of **one** word only which can be used appropriately in all three sentences. In this exercise, the words required can be found in the reading extracts on page 31 and 32 of the Coursebook. Here is an example (**0**).

**0** The chef complained that everyone was **getting in his** ___way___ and ordered them to leave.

Ron is determined to win this competition and I can't imagine him **going out of his** ___way___ to help anyone else.

I was surprised that none of the people I asked **knew the** ___way___ **to** the museum.

**1** The headmaster must **take** urgent ____________ to stop the bullying that is happening in this school.

I had to stop and rest before I climbed the final ___________ of the lighthouse.

If you get lost in the woods, you should **retrace your** _________ and go back to camp.

**2** The group believed the song __________ **a good chance of** being a hit but didn't dream it would reach number 1.

Being the only child with an American accent, I _________ **out** amongst the other children at school.

My parents __________ **by me** all the time I was in prison and did everything they could to get me released.

**3** **Would you** ________ **for** a cup of coffee while you're waiting to see Mr Williams?

Our society should **take** more __________ **of** the elderly and treat them with respect.

Martin doesn't seem to ________ that his aggressive behaviour could get him into trouble.

**4** Police now doubt that anyone will __________ **responsibility** for the bomb that exploded yesterday.

The old lady's ___________ that she had seen a UFO was never taken seriously by anyone.

If you have an accident and **make a** ______________, you will have to pay more for future car insurance.

**5** Ministers have been told to wait until the Foreign Secretary _________ **a** formal **statement** before speaking to the press about the incident.

The subject of legalizing drugs is one of those **controversial** __________which is unlikely to be resolved soon.

In the next two___________ of the National Reporter we will be bringing you a special report on the health care crisis.

# Writing

CAE Part 1

## Formal letters

1 Read the following Writing Part 1 task. Before you write your answer, do the related tasks in **A–C** below the question.

You are studying at a college in the Parkdale area of Blatchington. You have read a newspaper article about a proposal to close the local library. Read the article, on which you have made some notes, and the results of a survey carried out by your class. Then write a **letter** to the newspaper editor, responding to the article and explaining why you feel the library should not be closed.

## 'Library should close,' says councillor

LOCAL COUNCILLOR David Markham has called for the closure of the public library in Blatchington's Parkdale area. According to Mr Markham the Parkdale library is <u>underused</u>, with most residents preferring the larger <u>Central Library in Green Street</u>. 'A <u>great deal of money has been injected into the Parkdale library</u>,' explained Councillor Markham, 'yet local residents have failed to take advantage of the facilities. The building could be <u>converted into a sports facility</u>.'

*nonsense! Not what our survey says*

*too far for many*

*where's the proof?*

*more important to have a decent library*

**Class survey of Parkdale residents**

How often do you use the Parkdale library?

| | | | |
|---|---|---|---|
| At least three times a week | 9% | About once a month | 41% |
| Once or twice a week | 38% | Never | 12% |

Write your **letter** in **180–220** words. You do not need to include postal addresses.

**A Summarizing the information in the survey**

Which of the following sentences would be more appropriate for your letter? Why?

1 *In our survey 9% of the people we interviewed use the Parkdale library at least three times a week, 38% use it once or twice a week, 41% go there about once a month and only 12% never use it.*

2 *Almost half of those residents interviewed visit the library at least once a week and only a relatively small percentage said they make no use of its facilities at all.*

**B Using your own words**

Where possible you should avoid copying the language contained in the input material. Complete each of the gaps in sentences **1–4** with one of the nouns from the box. Then match each sentence to the handwritten note on the newspaper article which it expresses.

| journey | claim | evidence | priority |
|---|---|---|---|

1 __________ should be given to the improvement of the existing service.

2 A large number of residents are unable to make the long __________ into the town centre.

3 Your __________ that local residents do not use the library is untrue.

4 There is little __________ of this investment.

**C Building on the information**

Successful answers expand on one or two of the points in the input material. Make notes answering each of the questions below.

1 *too far for many*
What types of people might find it difficult to travel into the town centre?

2 *where's the proof?*
What evidence might there be to prove a *lack* of investment in the library?

3 *more important to have a decent library*
Why is a library important? And why is a new sports facility less important?

You are told to write 180–220 words, so you may not be able to use all your ideas.

**Don't forget!**

- Your letter should be consistently formal.
- See pages 21 and 194 of the Coursebook for information on writing formal letters.

# 4 Work time

## Reading

CAE Part 3

### Multiple choice

You are going to read a magazine article about work and holidays. For questions **1–7**, choose the answer **(A**, **B**, **C** or **D)** which you think fits best according to the text.

## No cure for the summertime blues

*Paul Gould looks at the highs of going away and the lows as your post-holiday glow fades.*

Irrespective of the destination, it's the coming back that hurts. As you trudge in to work and go back to the old routine, post-holiday blues hit whether you've been to a tropical paradise or simply spent a week at a local campsite. It is a recognized psychological pattern: we switch to a low after a high, we get despondent when a spell of basking in bliss is abruptly ended.

For me, that bliss was tasted at its most intoxicating two years ago in a secluded bay in southern Crete in Greece. At the time, a fortnight seemed to expand into a way of life. Days were taken up with massage, sunbathing, swimming and yoga. There was constant laughter amongst friends. Being a wage-slave seemed inconceivable: I was born to dance and sing and be pampered. This, I felt, was how life should be. More unsettling, though, was my conviction that life could be like this. If only I could cling on to this happy state, my potential for joy and creativity would be unlocked.

It couldn't last. The blues set in even before the holiday ended. What we needed, one of our group declared, was a post-holiday trauma support group. Is trauma too strong a word? Cary Cooper, professor of psychology at the University of Manchester, says the symptoms are undoubtedly genuine: 'It's things like being more aggressive or more withdrawn, mild depression, feeling tired even after a good night's sleep. Really, you're angry at the lifestyle you're re-entering but you can't take it out on your lifestyle so you take it out on other people.'

So what of my hope of clinging on to that holiday feeling? My resolutions were to continue yoga classes, to take up massage and to rise above stress. Couldn't I maintain that way of life? 'The reason you don't is that people get really absorbed in work, then get on the train or whatever, and by the time they get home they're exhausted and just flop in front of the TV,' says Professor Cooper. The post-holiday glow may last a day or two. There's the gratification of colleagues asking where you've been. It can be quite amusing for the first morning when you can show off by telling people you've been to exciting places having more fun than them. But then day-to-day hassles crowd in thick and fast. The holiday may well have seemed like ages at the time, but now it shrinks to a tiny blip. You feel cheated.

Perhaps holidays give us an unrealistic taste of fantasy. I detect something altogether darker: they compel us to see how much aggravation, tedium and mediocrity we put up with the rest of the time. On a more paranoid note, is it possible we've been intoxicated by a cynical holidays industry? Are holidays just a mechanism whereby we swap our role as producers in the great big economic machine for that of the consumer? Professor Cooper confirms my fears: 'We go on holiday and become consumers and because work is so time-consuming, the way we justify it is to use the money to make us feel better about our limited existence, saying: "At least I can afford a nice holiday".' Surely we can't just blame the industry? Some of my best holidays have simply been times when I chose to hang out with friends, have long conversations, feel carefree. Professor Cooper believes these are opportunities that allow us to invest in relationships.

After a holiday, Professor Cooper advises going back to work gradually: 'Do only the stuff that needs immediate attention, leave on time, go to the gym.' Thank goodness work–life balance has entered public debate. It is high time we got agitated about the realisation that four weeks' holiday a year and a working week of 40 hours plus means we can set aside no time or energy for things that matter, such as our partners, our children, our friends, staying healthy, or cooking instead of ready meals. But Professor Cooper's advice so far can only help so much. A more revolutionary solution is downshifting. 'People see the gap between a normal human life and the treadmill existence and realize the cost is too great,' he says. 'So they think: "Why not work for a smaller company or set up on my own?"'

Yet the long-hours culture is probably only part of the problem. That post-exotica depression is also brought on by sheer boredom, noisy neighbours or, worse, domestic issues causing tension. The traditional saying is 'There's no place like home' but it sometimes seems there's no place like away from it all. In his acclaimed book *The Art of Travel*, Alain de Botton sums up this yearning: 'Few seconds in life are more releasing than those in which a plane ascends to the sky … its ascent is a symbol of transformation. It can inspire us to imagine analogous, decisive shifts in our own lives; to imagine that we too might one day surge above much that looms over us.' So perhaps the only way to cure post-holiday blues is to start planning the next one as soon as you get back.

**1** In paragraph one, the writer suggests that post-holiday feelings of depression
**A** occur when a holiday has been cut short.
**B** happen regardless of the holiday location.
**C** arise when a holiday has not been satisfying.
**D** affect people with little variation in their work.

**2** During his holiday in Crete, the writer was
**A** resentful about an illusion of happiness.
**B** certain he could maintain that way of living.
**C** determined to start working for himself.
**D** astonished at the change in his behaviour.

**3** What does Professor Cary Cooper believe about trauma?
**A** People have a tendency to confuse stress with trauma.
**B** It has a serious impact on performance at work.
**C** Holidays can only increase trauma which already exists in a person.
**D** It can cause people to behave in an unpleasant way towards others.

**4** What are we told about people who have been back at work for a few days?
**A** They feel as though the holiday they had was too short.
**B** They exaggerate when describing it to their colleagues.
**C** They lack the mental discipline to maintain a lifestyle change.
**D** They underestimate the time they need to commit to work.

**5** In paragraph five, the writer states that going on holiday forces people to
**A** focus on relationships they have neglected.
**B** be keener to assert their superior social status.
**C** recognize the frustrations of everyday life.
**D** work longer hours in order to afford time off.

**6** In paragraph six, one of the writer's aims is to
**A** encourage people to protest about their working hours.
**B** persuade people of the value of personal relationships.
**C** highlight which of Professor Cooper's proposals are valid.
**D** illustrate the advantages of people becoming self-employed.

**7** The writer's purpose in using the quotation from *The Art of Travel* is to
**A** contrast people's dreams with what they actually go on to achieve.
**B** promote the idea that risk-takers lead a more rewarding life.
**C** discourage people from settling down before they are ready.
**D** show the pleasure derived from dreaming about a different lifestyle.

# Vocabulary

Wordlist on page 211 of the Coursebook.

## A Adjectives of personality

Match each of the adjectives to an appropriate description.

| | | | |
|---|---|---|---|
| slapdash | approachable | attentive | trustworthy |
| industrious | domineering | single-minded | conceited |

1 She always works very hard. ______________
2 He doesn't take much care over his work. ______________
3 She's so friendly and easy to talk to. ______________
4 He thinks he's so intelligent – it's extremely irritating. ______________
5 The staff are always so polite and helpful. ______________
6 Her only aim is to become managing director. ______________
7 Your secret is safe with her. ______________
8 He tries to control others without any consideration for their feelings or opinions. ______________

## B Time

Complete each of the gaps with one of the words from the box.

| | | | | |
|---|---|---|---|---|
| at | aside | for | of | in |
| to | out | on | off | up |

1 Sorry, I can't stop to chat – I'm a little **pressed** _____ **time**.
2 We had hoped to discuss the matter in the meeting but we **ran** _____ **of time**.
3 I always try to **set** _____ **some time** each day to read the newspaper.
4 We have a huge garden, which **takes** _____ **most of my free time**.
5 Not many people have heard of her, but **it's only a matter** _____ **time before** she becomes famous.
6 I did as much as I could _____ **the time available**.
7 We didn't arrange to meet _____ **any specific time**, but I'm surprised he's not here yet.
8 He is retiring from his post in order to **devote more time** _____ his family.
9 She always gets straight to the point; she doesn't like to **waste time** _____ small talk.
10 All pregnant women in this country have the right to **take time** _____ **work** for antenatal care.

### Self help

Add the expressions in bold in B to your vocabulary notebook.

## C Skills

Complete the crossword by solving the anagrams. Each answer is a single-word item of vocabulary which collocates with the word **skills**. The first one has been done for you.

**Across**

**4** mop truce
**8** lice chant
**10** comic mountain
**11** rose plan

**Down**

**1** pen to heel
**2** an ailing rat zoo
**3** arctic pal
**5** busses in
**6** a secret rail
**7** a mail range
**9** a lung age

## Language focus

Grammar reference on page 218 of the Coursebook.

### Punctuation

Each line in the following article contains a punctuation mistake. Correct the mistakes. There is an example at the beginning **(0)**.

**0** A heating company near Birmingham has introduced group hugs to ~~it's~~ its workforce
**1** in a drive to boost staff morale. Since, employees at Farrelly Engineering started
**2** hugging first thing in the morning and last thing at night; profits have more than
**3** doubled Now the firm is introducing other initiatives, including soothing music
**4** and regular nights' out at company expense. The idea came after Jerry Farrelly,
**5** the director went on a motivational course in an attempt to improve morale. He
**6** explained, that while many of his staff were suspicious at first, they soon came to
**7** appreciate the regime. Often new staff raise their eyebrows when they see what
**8** goes on, but we have found they soon get into the mood,' he said. Padma Mistry
**9** who works in the accounts-department, commented on the difference between the
**10** attitudes of men and women, 'The girls decided among themselves to start hugging
**11** each other,' she explained. 'The men dont want to join in, but they have tried to
**12** shake each others hands each day. A hug is a superb start to the day. We never
**13** argue now as everything is so relaxed. Its a really fun place to work.' Rob Carter,
**14** who has worked for the firm for five years said he used to work long hours and get
**15** very stressed. However that's all changed. 'It may sound strange, but I actually look
**16** forward to going in to work on Monday now, he confessed.'

# Use of English

## CAE Part 2

### Open cloze

For questions **1–15**, read the text below and think of the word which best fits each gap. Use only **one** word in each gap. There is an example at the beginning **(0)**.

**Don't forget!**

- Read the text through first before you start to make your choices.
- The emphasis is on grammatical words, such as prepositions, auxiliary verbs and articles.

### Female butlers

A new breed of butlers has appeared **(0)** _on_ the scene; increasingly, it seems **(1)** ______ rich and famous are turning **(2)** ______ women to perform the little domestic duties of everyday life. But **(3)** ______ female butlers are in ever greater demand, they are also in short supply. Ivor Spencer, who runs the **(4)** ______ traditional of the well known butler schools, **(5)** ______ trained only eight women in 21 years. Even at the more progressive butler academies, **(6)** ______ as Robert Watson's Guild of Professional Butlers, fewer than one **(7)** ______ four trainees are female.

Butlerine Sarah Whittle says that women are in demand **(8)** ______ they're less stuffy than men. 'We're better **(9)** ______ picking up on people's moods,' she says. 'And we can organize several things at **(10)** ______ : it's in our nature to multitask.' Whittle **(11)** ______ expected to be smart and professional **(12)** ______ duty, but she does get glamorous perks – presents of chocolate, champagne and, on **(13)** ______ occasion, an expensive pair of shoes. But the job has its downside. Hundred-hour weeks are **(14)** ______ uncommon, the hours are unsociable and the tasks often **(15)** ______ than glamorous.

## CAE Part 3

### Word formation

For questions **1–10**, use the word given in capitals at the end of some of the lines to form a word that fits in the gap **in the same line**. There is an example at the beginning **(0)**.

### Sales manager

As part of its major new programme of **(0)** _expansion_ RAL Cosmetics is seeking to **EXPAND**
appoint a dynamic sales professional to run a team of sales **(1)** ____________ in **REPRESENT**
the UK. You will be highly-motivated, with the drive and **(2)** ____________ to be the **DETERMINE**
best in your field. You will also have strong **(3)** ____________ qualities and be an **LEAD**
effective communicator. The position will involve frequent travel to Europe for
**(4)** ____________ at international sales conferences, as well as training courses at **ATTEND**
our head office in Lyon. Priority will be given to those **(5)** ____________ who can **APPLY**
demonstrate a good working knowledge of French. Previous experience in the cosmetics
industry is **(6)** ____________ though not essential. We guarantee a comprehensive and **PREFER**
**(7)** ____________ remuneration package, including a company car, private health **COMPETE**
**(8)** ____________ and a contributory pension scheme. If you feel you have the necessary **INSURE**
qualities and background, and enjoy working in a **(9)** ____________, high-paced **CHALLENGE**
environment, send your CV to Alain Sylvestre, 22 rue Marivaux, 69142 Lyon, France.
Closing date for **(10)** ____________ of applications: September 25th. **RECEIVE**

CAE Part 5

## Key word transformations: gerunds and infinitives

Complete the second sentence so that it has a similar meaning to the first sentence, using the word given. **Do not change the word given**. You must use between **three** and **six** words, including the word given. Here is an example **(0)**.

**0** She will often panic if there is a problem.
**TENDENCY**
She _has a tendency to panic in_ the face of a problem.

**1** I was surprised when he said he wouldn't work overtime.
**REFUSAL**
His ______________________ as a surprise to me.

**2** Don't bother to read that book.
**WORTH**
It ______________________ that book.

**3** Shall I carry your bag for you?
**LIKE**
Would ______________________ your bag for you?

**4** He tried very hard to stop smoking.
**EFFORT**
He ______________________ up smoking.

**5** I found it impossible not to laugh when he said that.
**HELP**
I ______________________ when he said that.

**6** If you don't leave now, you'll miss the bus.
**BETTER**
You ______________________ else you'll miss the bus.

**7** I find it difficult to remember names.
**DIFFICULTY**
I ______________________ names.

**8** They made us clean up the mess.
**MADE**
We ______________________ up the mess.

**9** She didn't like the fact that he had been treated so badly.
**BEING**
She objected ______________________ so badly.

# Writing

CAE Part 2

## Reports

1 Read the following Writing Part 2 task.

An international research group is carrying out an investigation into changing trends in the way young people spend their free time. You have been asked to write a report about the situation in your country. You should:

- describe the changes that have taken place over the last twenty years in the way that young people spend their free time
- say whether these changes have been for the better or the worse
- suggest how you think the situation might develop in the future.

Write your **report** in **220–260** words.

2 The following report was written in answer to the task above by a British person **in the mid-1960s**. Put the paragraphs in the correct order, using the underlined words to help you. Then write a suitable heading for each paragraph.

### Young people's leisure time activities

**1** ..................................................................

<u>The growth in popularity of the car</u> has made once popular pastimes rather dangerous. Street games such as football, skipping or marbles are no longer such a common sight. Similarly, cycling on the open road is becoming less attractive, particularly with the construction of motorways, which began at the end of the last decade. Sadly, youngsters now spend more time in the home, where <u>another invention</u> has radically transformed their habits.

**2** ..................................................................

<u>The main difference between now and twenty years ago</u> is the increased wealth and greater amount of free time available to young people. This, in itself, represents a welcome change, but <u>two other developments</u> have restricted the nature and quality of leisure time activities.

**3** ..................................................................

It is highly likely that <u>television will continue to dominate the lives of our youth</u> in the years to come. Teenagers and people in their twenties may well spend most of their spare time at home, simply watching TV programmes or listening to their latest long-playing records. They might even begin to wish they had less free time on their hands.

**4** ..................................................................

<u>The purpose of this report is</u> to comment on recent changes in the way young people make use of their spare time in my country and to consider possible future trends.

**5** ..................................................................

Where previously whole families would gather round the radio to listen to a gripping drama, now children fight with their parents over which of the two <u>television</u> channels they should select. Courting couples rarely go ballroom dancing or join long queues outside cinemas and music halls as they once did; instead, <u>they stay in to watch television</u> or perhaps worse, attend wild pop concerts or parties, where they dance in uncontrolled ways.

3 Find examples in the model of the following:

| Language used to compare the past and the present | Different ways of referring to young people |
| --- | --- |
| eg *once popular pastimes* | eg *youngsters* |
| **Language used to make future predictions** | **Different ways of referring to free time** |
| eg *It is highly likely that television will continue ...* | |

4 Underline those words and expressions which express the writer's opinion on whether the changes have been for the better or the worse.

eg *This, in itself, represents a welcome change ...*

5 The writer of the report uses a consistently formal register. Sometimes, this involves using nouns rather than verbs. For each of the following, find the equivalent expression in the model answer.

**a** The car has become more and more popular ...

______________________________

**b** ... especially because they've built motorways ...

______________________________

**c** ... young people have more money and more free time.

______________________________

6 Now write your own answer to the question on page 34.

## Useful language

Refer to the following sections in the Wordlist of the Coursebook:

- Possibility: page 209
- Change: page 210

## Don't forget!

- Plan your answer before you write.
- Use a consistently formal register.
- Link one paragraph with the next, as in the model.
- Give your report a title and each of your paragraphs a heading.

# 5 Getting on

## Reading

CAE Part 1

### Multiple choice

You are going to read three extracts which are all concerned in some way with relationships. For questions **1–6**, choose the answer **(A**, **B**, **C** or **D)** which you think fits best according to the text.

### Homestay Families required for Overseas Students

GLOBAL LANGUAGES are currently seeking potential families who could offer homestay accommodation to our students. Being a homestay provider means offering accommodation to one or more students (one room per student) from two weeks up to a six-month duration. Families may opt for providing board and lodging over Christmas, for which they would receive a 20% supplement. Both homestay families and overseas students are required to complete a detailed questionnaire regarding their preferences and requirements to ensure successful placements. Prior to being registered as one of our families, it is essential that you agree to socialize with your students for a minimum of two hours per evening and six hours over the weekend. A homestay co-ordinator can be contacted 24 hours a day in case of emergency.

Our students are of diverse nationalities and come to England with a view to improving their English, but also to discover England's many cultural attractions. They tend to be independent-minded and prefer to organize trips and outings individually or with their peer group. You may also find that they will often eat out, although they are advised to notify their homestay family if they do not require an evening meal. Homestay providers who receive the most positive feed-back are the ones who allow their students to integrate within their family. It is the opportunity for this kind of relationship which usually makes students go for the homestay experience and why we offer this kind of accommodation.

**1** To be accepted as a homestay provider, a family must
- **A** be able to offer accommodation during public holidays.
- **B** accept any student that the school allocates to them.
- **C** take responsibility for a student in urgent situations.
- **D** be willing to spend a set amount of time with their students.

**2** Students tend to choose the homestay option because they
- **A** want to feel they are part of a family.
- **B** do not wish to arrange excursions by themselves.
- **C** are anxious about living alone in a foreign country.
- **D** have no time to prepare their own food.

## Extract from novel

"Sometimes I regret that I ever married into a Chinese family," Phil said when he heard we had to go to San Francisco, a hundred miles round-trip from our house in San Jose, made worse by weekend football traffic. Although he's become genuinely fond of my mother over the fifteen years we've been married, he's still exasperated by her demands. And a weekend with the extended family is definitely not his preferred way to spend his days off from the hospital. "Are you sure we have to go?" he said absently. He was busy playing with a new software program he had just loaded onto his laptop computer. He pressed a key. "Hotcha!"* he exclaimed to the screen, and clapped his hands. Phil is forty-three years old and with his wiry gray hair he usually strikes most people as reserved and dignified. At that moment, however, he had the pure intensity of a little boy playing with a battleship.

I pretended to be equally busy, perusing the help-wanted section. Three months ago, I took a position as a speech and language clinician with the local school district. And while I was basically happy with the job I secretly worried I had missed a better opportunity. My mother had put those thoughts in my head. Right after I announced I had been chosen over two other candidates for the same position, she said, "Two? Only two people wanted that job?"

* Hotcha is slang expressing delight or success.

**3** The writer refers to 'a little boy playing with a battleship' in order to
- **A** emphasise Phil's lack of maturity.
- **B** show a different side of Phil's character.
- **C** suggest that Phil misspends his time.
- **D** imply that Phil is ignoring her.

**4** After the writer had told her mother about her job, she
- **A** felt that her mother was in some way envious of her.
- **B** was concerned she had not looked for another position.
- **C** decided she was in the wrong field of work.
- **D** wished she had kept it secret from her mother.

## Machine rage is dead ... long live emotional computing

You have spent the last 20 minutes talking to an automated call centre. A passionless, computerized voice drones out assurances and urges you to press yet another key. Your blood pressure soars. Finally you hurl your phone at the wall. Or your teenage son becomes immersed, with increasing agitation, in a computer game. As his temper worsens, his performance declines until he ends up trashing the console in a fit of adolescent rage. Computer angst – now a universal feature of modern life – is an expensive business when you come to think of it!

Fortunately, the days of the unfeeling machine will soon be over. Thanks to breakthroughs in artificial intelligence, psychology, electronics and other research fields, scientists are now creating computers and robots that can detect, and respond to, users' feelings. The discoveries are being channelled by *Humaine*, a £6 million programme that has just been launched by the European Union to give Europe a lead in emotional computing. As a result, computers will soon detect our growing irritation at their behaviour and in turn generate more sympathetic, human-like messages or slow down the tempo of the games they are running. Robots will be able to react in lifelike ways, though we may end up releasing some unwelcome creations too. 'Computers that can detect and imitate human emotion may sound like science fiction, but they are already with us,' said Dr Dylan Evans, a key *Humaine* project collaborator.

**5** What does the writer feel is the problem with modern technology?
- **A** It does not function in the intended way.
- **B** It tends to cause friction between family members.
- **C** It can result in people losing their self-control.
- **D** It is impossible to achieve anything without technology.

**6** What are we told about computers and robots in the second paragraph?
- **A** Computers will be able to adjust their behaviour to human need.
- **B** Robots may have superior social skills compared to some people.
- **C** Computers will be uniquely programmed to respond to individual users.
- **D** Europe has recently taken the lead in developments in technology.

## Vocabulary

Wordlist on page 211 of the Coursebook.

### Adjective and noun collocations

1 Match each of the nouns in the box to one of the groups of adjectives **1–8**. All the adjectives in the group must collocate with the noun.

| |
|---|
| relationship |
| argument |
| love |
| feelings |
| family |
| friend |
| couple |
| tension |

| | | | | | |
|---|---|---|---|---|---|
| **1** | brotherly | first | true | unrequited | ________ |
| **2** | inner | mixed | negative | strong | ________ |
| **3** | courting | elderly | married | young | ________ |
| **4** | close | love-hate | rocky | stable | ________ |
| **5** | best | close | mutual | school | ________ |
| **6** | adoptive | extended | immediate | single-parent | ________ |
| **7** | heated | furious | fierce | pointless | ________ |
| **8** | family | social | rising | heightened | ________ |

2 Complete each of the gaps with an appropriate adjective from exercise 1.

**1** I have a ____________ **relationship** with my job; how I feel about it usually depends on what mood I'm in when I get to work.

**2** It was a ____________ **argument**: neither of us was ever likely to change the other's way of thinking.

**3** Her latest novel is a tale of ____________ **love**; Ross is besotted with his boss Hermione, who shows no interest in her young admirer.

**4** Sandra's parents have ____________ **feelings** about her going to live abroad; they want her to lead her own life, but they'd be happier if she did so closer to home.

**5** We're not inviting any aunts or uncles and so on – just the ____________ **family**.

**6** I met Paul on holiday and he's become quite a ____________ **friend**.

**7** The photograph shows a young ____________ **couple** speaking to a priest, probably about their forthcoming wedding.

**8** Faced with mounting ____________ **tension**, the government introduced a number of far-reaching political reforms.

## Language focus

G Grammar reference on page 220 of the Coursebook.

### Relative clauses

Correct the following sentences by changing the underlined word. You should write only **one** word.

**1** We thought it was horrible, so we gave it to my mother, she loves that kind of thing.

**2** The plane took off over two hours late, what meant I missed my connecting flight in Frankfurt.

**3** He was criticized for giving a speech on a subject about that he knew very little.

**4** There are two or three people in the photo which name I can't remember.

**5** We're going back to the same hotel that we stayed last year.

**6** I still don't understand the reason because they decided to close the sports centre.

**7** My eldest son, that lives in Japan now, hardly ever comes back to visit us.

**8** Kate and Steve were the only two people from work to came to our wedding.

## Alternatives to relative clauses

**1** Infinitives with 'to' can be used:

- after words like *someone, nobody, anything* etc.

*There is* ***nothing to suggest*** *that the crimes are connected.* (= *nothing which suggests*)

- to replace relative clauses containing a modal verb.

*There are* ***several dishes to choose from.*** (= *several dishes which you can choose from*)

- after phrases like *the first, the next, the only* and superlatives.

***The next person to talk*** *will get extra homework.* (= *the next person who talks*)
*He has become* ***the oldest person ever to run*** *a marathon.* (= *the oldest person who has ever run*)

**2** Relative clauses can be reduced by using:

- a present participle

***Anyone wanting*** *further information, should contact Peter Wiley.* (= *Anyone who wants*)
*Who's that* ***person sitting*** *next to your brother?* (= *person who is sitting*)

- a past participle.

*The two* ***men arrested*** *in connection with the robbery have been released without charge.* (= *men who were/had been arrested*)

1 Which famous siblings are described in each of the following pairs of sentences?

**1 a** They are not the only sisters ever to play each other in the final of a Wimbledon championship.
**b** Venus was champion in 2000 and 2001, but Serena was the one to collect the winner's trophy in 2002.

**2 a** When Michael was four, his father gave him a go-kart powered by a lawnmower engine.
**b** After a race, Ralf was usually the first to phone his mother.

**3 a** Some of their most famous films are *Monkey Business, Duck Soup* and *A Night at the Opera*, all released in the 1930s.
**b** One of the five brothers 'wore' a moustache painted on with black greasepaint; he found it easier than glueing one on.

**4 a** Fans hoping to see Janet in concert were disappointed to hear that she had cancelled her planned tour.
**b** Michael began his musical career at the age of five as the lead singer of a group comprising himself and four of his eight brothers and sisters.

**5 a** John was the youngest man ever to be elected President, and he was also the youngest to die.
**b** The biography does not make it clear whether Robert, known affectionately as Bobby, had evidence to back up his suspicions that the CIA had killed his brother.

2 Rewrite the underlined parts of the above sentences using relative pronouns.

***Example*: 1 a** the only sisters who have ever played each other

# Use of English

CAE Part 4

## Gapped sentences

For questions **1–5**, think of **one** word only which can be used appropriately in all three sentences. Here is an example **(0)**.

**0** The other children would often laugh at her, _call_ **her names** and make her cry.

Alan Kelcher was very laid-back, and let his pupils _call_ **him by his first name.**

**Give her a** _call_ and ask her to go out with you.

**1** House prices ______ **dramatically** last year and they bought themselves a small flat near the town centre.

I always thought that love at first sight only happened in films but I ______ **for** Jill the moment I set eyes on her.

He ______ **out with** his father after a blazing row and hasn't spoken to him since.

**2** The President highlighted the ______ **relationship** that existed between the two countries, who, he said, were now 'the closest of allies'.

Relations with management have not improved and there's a ______ **chance** the unions will call a strike next week.

I never liked kissing my grandmother, because I couldn't stand the ______ **smell** of her perfume.

**3** He had a friendly, open face and she ______ **an instant liking to** him.

In appearance Emily ______ **after** her father, but she inherited her intelligence from her mother.

It ______ some **time to** sort out our marriage problems, but now our relationship is pretty good.

**4** They've had **a** ______ **of** disagreements recently, but normally they get on fine together.

Can you reverse the car a little more so we can ______ it **to** the caravan?

The whole restaurant had been booked by a middle-aged **married** ______ celebrating their silver wedding anniversary.

**5** His latest novel centres on the uneasy relationship between the two countries **at the** ______ **of the last century**.

The last person I expected to ______ **up** at our wedding was my ex-boyfriend!

I usually ______ **to** my mother **for** help or advice: she's a better listener than my father.

CAE Part 1

## Multiple-choice cloze

For questions **1–12**, read the text below and decide which answer **(A**, **B**, **C** or **D)** best fits each gap. There is an example at the beginning **(0)**.

### Dutch children enjoy their freedom

'Let them be free' is the **(0)** ________ rule for child-rearing in the Netherlands. No wonder Dutch kids have been **(1)** ________ Europe's most fortunate by a recent UNICEF survey. From a tender age, their opinions are **(2)** ________, their wishes respected, and there is no homework until their last year in preparatory school. Some would **(3)** ________ that the tendency of Dutch society to encourage infants to experience whatever they please has **(4)** ________ a whole generation into spoilt, undisciplined brats. Others say family members are remarkably **(5)** ________ with one another, feeling free to say anything, and that the way parents **(6)** ________ with their children's anxieties means that the children are well-adjusted, which is **(7)** ________ up by the results of the survey.

Dr Gerrit Breeusma, head of development psychology at the University of Groningen says the survey's results came as no **(8)** ________. 'Children have always played a very important role in Holland but there were **(9)** ________ within families during the Sixties, usually over matters of discipline and conformity. As a result, the generation growing up at that time have made sure they **(10)** ________ on better with their kids,' he added.

However, in several Dutch police precincts, such liberalism is not viewed positively. In an attempt to **(11)** ________ underage heavy drinking, police have taken to bringing home teenagers and threatening parents with obligatory attendance at courses on excessive alcohol problems or hefty fines unless they keep their children under **(12)** ________ .

| | | | | |
|---|---|---|---|---|
| **0** | **A** <u>golden</u> | **B** iron | **C** solid | **D** fixed |
| **1** | **A** compared | **B** put | **C** rated | **D** assessed |
| **2** | **A** regarded | **B** valued | **C** recognized | **D** measured |
| **3** | **A** argue | **B** criticize | **C** defend | **D** judge |
| **4** | **A** resulted | **B** created | **C** brought | **D** turned |
| **5** | **A** alike | **B** open | **C** true | **D** careful |
| **6** | **A** empathize | **B** understand | **C** analyse | **D** handle |
| **7** | **A** shown | **B** held | **C** made | **D** backed |
| **8** | **A** doubt | **B** difference | **C** consequence | **D** surprise |
| **9** | **A** beliefs | **B** conflicts | **C** decisions | **D** contradictions |
| **10** | **A** follow | **B** carry | **C** get | **D** continue |
| **11** | **A** tackle | **B** supervise | **C** extinguish | **D** dispose |
| **12** | **A** control | **B** limits | **C** restriction | **D** rule |

# Writing

CAE Part 2

## Essay

1 Read the following Writing Part 2 task.

You have recently had a class debate, in which students discussed whether knowledge or social connections were more useful in achieving success. Your teacher has asked you to write an essay, giving your opinion on the following statement.

*It's not what you know, but who you know that counts.*

Write your **essay** in **220–260** words.

2 What does the statement above mean? Do you have a similar saying in your language?

3 Read the following sample answer and decide which of the following sentences **a–c** best summarizes the author's point of view.

**a** Generally speaking, people rely more on their social connections than their knowledge.
**b** Knowledge is more useful in the long-term than having the right social connections.
**c** Wealthy people benefit from making social connections and poorer people benefit from knowledge.

This is an English saying which has an equivalent in many languages. Indeed, a major reason for mankind's global existence today is that humans rely on one another for survival. <u>However</u> **(1)**, humans also have a brain capable of storing a great deal of information. <u>To what extent</u> **(2)**, then, is knowledge of less importance than social connections?

Some would argue that knowing the 'right' person is the key to success. An example of this is when people are only accepted into social circles due to their relationship with 'VIPs': <u>in other words</u> **(3)** by knowing the right person, you can gain entry into golf clubs, exclusive restaurants and so on. <u>Furthermore</u> **(4)**, in certain cultures, it is common practice for parents to request that acquaintances or relatives in positions of power find work for a son or daughter.

I personally believe, however, that a person must have the right knowledge to do their work successfully. You cannot rely on an employer's goodwill forever if you are not performing well. <u>In most cases</u> **(5)**, getting ahead at work requires intelligence and a natural aptitude for the job. <u>Likewise</u> **(6)**, successful academic performance requires in-depth knowledge of a subject. <u>Admittedly</u> **(7)**, it sometimes happens that certain weak students are assessed more favourably than they deserve because their parents have 'friends in the right places', but eventually they will have to prove their true ability in the real world.

In conclusion, <u>while</u> **(8)** it may be true that knowing the right people can allow you to obtain what you desire more quickly, it is knowledge that will allow you to hold on to it.

4 Which of the three paragraph plans, **A**, **B** or **C**, on page 68 of the Coursebook does the essay follow?

5 Match the underlined words and phrases **1–8** in the sample answer to explanations **a–h**.

This word/phrase ...

**a** means 'in the same or similar way'.

**b** could be replaced with 'In general'.

**c** is used to say that you agree that something is true, although it may make your main idea weaker.

**d** is used to add an additional idea, statement or example to the previous one.

**e** could be replaced with 'how much'.

**f** is used to introduce a contrasting point to the previous statement.

**g** can be replaced with 'Although'.

**h** is followed by an explanation of the previous statement.

6 Write an essay giving your opinion on **one** of the following statements.

**1** Young people should be taught that participation and team work is more important than winning.

**2** Young people today have much easier lives than young people did a generation ago.

**3** Details of people's private lives have no place in a national newspaper.

**4** Work cannot be truly satisfying unless it is well paid.

**5** It is inadvisable to get married before your mid-twenties.

## Before you write

- Each numbered statement in exercise 6 deals with a theme from Units 1–5 of the Coursebook. When you have chosen which essay you are going to write, look back at the unit with the same number and note down any vocabulary you could use in your answer.
- Choose one of the paragraph plans A, B or C on p68 of the Coursebook.
- Make notes about the content of each paragraph before you write the essay.
- Decide which of the phrases and expressions on pages 69 and 197 of the Coursebook you could use.

# 6 All in the mind?

## Reading

CAE Part 4

### Multiple matching

1 Read paragraphs **1** and **2**. In these paragraphs, the writer's tone shows that she is probably

**a** sceptical regarding the use of dogs in the classroom.

**b** impressed with Henry's effect on the children.

**c** unconvinced that Henry is making any difference.

2 You are going to read a newspaper article about the effect of having a dog in the classroom. For questions **1–15**, choose from the paragraphs **(A–G)**. The paragraphs may be chosen more than once.

**In which paragraph are the following mentioned?**

a way that students can overcome their fear of making mistakes **1** ____

the criteria regarding the selection of an appropriate dog **2** ____

the claim that a dog has increased the students' attendance at school **3** ____

a motivating reason for students to keep up with their school work **4** ____

evidence to back up the theory that dogs can improve physical well-being **5** ____

the celebrity status that a dog has recently acquired **6** ____

people eventually being persuaded that a dog at school is beneficial **7** ____

a misunderstanding concerning the treatment of a dog **8** ____

a dog's popularity not attracting negative feelings **9** ____

the inability to explain how a dog can have a relaxing effect **10** ____

the writer's belief that young people are unwilling to talk about their problems **11** ____

a decision which was taken to avoid provoking people **12** ____

the accusation that schools have dogs just to attract media attention **13** ____

a welcome positive effect on a group of people that Wendy Brown had not anticipated **14** ____

the fundamental reason why dogs can have a positive impact on people's happiness **15** ____

# Paws for thought

***Buying a dog for a school isn't a barking mad idea, says Mary Braid. Man's best friend is also a useful classroom assistant.***

**A** Henry is the undisputed star of Dronfield school near Sheffield. Whatever the achievements of other members of the comprehensive school, it is Henry with his soulful eyes and glossy hair, who has hogged the limelight, appearing on television in Britain and abroad. Yet despite all the public adulation, Henry stirs up no envy or resentment among the 2,000 students at Dronfield High – in fact, they all adore him. The pupils say the Cavalier King Charles spaniel is simply a pupil's best friend. Their teachers make even bigger assertions for Henry. They say the dog, who first arrived six months ago, is a super dog, who has improved pupil behaviour and encouraged more students to turn up regularly for their lessons and focus on their academic achievement.

**B** 'It's hard not to drift off in a large class sometimes,' explains Andrew Wainwright, 15, who like everyone else, is crazy about Henry. 'So when I go to catch-up classes, Henry is always in the room where they're held. He helps me focus and get on with it.' Andrew says Henry is a calming influence although he is unsure of why this might be. But he knows that there's something magical about being able to throw Henry a soft toy or have Henry lick his hand while he is studying. 'If we fall behind, Miss Brown won't let us look after him and everyone wants to walk Henry.'

**C** Wendy Brown is Andrew's teacher. It was Brown and Julie Smart, the school counsellor, who first proposed buying a school dog. 'Julie and I grew up with dogs and we were talking one day about how looking after dogs can affect children's conduct,' says Brown. 'We did some research and discovered that the presence of pets has been shown to be therapeutic. A number of studies have found that animals improve recovery after surgery or illness and have a calming influence on people in lots of settings. Some of my kids can be a handful and some of the children Julie counsels have terrible problems.'

**D** The two teachers could have plucked a dog from a rescue centre but felt that those dogs were more likely to have difficulties. What they and what troubled children needed was a stable, intelligent, people-loving animal. Step forward then puppy Henry, purchased from a local breeder. Julie looks after him after school hours – information that has calmed the animal lovers who complained to the school about Henry's treatment. 'They seemed to think we locked him in a school cupboard overnight,' says Brown. 'Also, the school budget was too tight to buy a dog and you can imagine that putting one before books might have stirred some people up a bit. We wanted the least controversy possible so we settled on approaching local churches. They donated the funds to buy him and his favourite food.'

**E** Today Henry is on Dronfield's front line when it comes to helping children struggling with everything from attention problems to a sudden death in the family. In the next few weeks, the dog will launch his own confidential counselling website, *Ask Henry*. Pupils will be encouraged to email and describe whatever is worrying them and Julie will answer on Henry's behalf. Wouldn't teenagers run horrified from such a scheme? Apparently not when Henry is involved! 'Henry has been a massive success,' insists Brown, explaining that even doubting staff have finally been won round. Perhaps that is because Henry, who lies on the floor during staff meetings, has also had a calming influence on teachers. 'Not part of the plan,' says Brown, 'but a very welcome benefit.'

**F** Could the school dog become a craze? Brown has already been contacted by eight schools keen to get their own dog. Other schools such as the Mulberry Bush, a primary school for 36 children with emotional and behavioural problems, have stepped forward to point out they already have one. Rosie Johnston, a Mulberry staff member, first brought her golden retriever, Muskoka, into school when he was just nine weeks old. That was three years ago. Aside from being a calming influence, Muskoka even plays his part in literacy lessons. Children at the school can be too shy to read to adults so they read to Muskoka. 'Their anxiety about mispronouncing something or getting the words in the wrong order is reduced when they read to him,' says Johnston.

**G** Psychologist Dr Deborah Wells from Queen's University Belfast specializes in animal-human interaction. She believes the underlying key to the Henry effect is that dogs offer unconditional love and that cheers up adults and children and helps with self-esteem. But traditionalist Chris Woodhead, the former chief inspector of schools says, 'I can see how children with behavioural difficulties might be helped but I'm sceptical about the use of dogs in mainstream education. I don't see why a teacher cannot create a positive learning environment through the subject they teach and their personality. Dogs strike me as a bit of a publicity stunt. It's the kind of sentimental story journalists love.' But Henry remains as popular as ever. He's just become the first animal to be made an honorary member of the public services union *Unison* – in recognition of his services as a canine classroom assistant.

## Vocabulary

Wordlist on page 212 of the Coursebook.

### A Sleep

| |
|---|
| off |
| into |
| on |
| over |
| from |
| through |
| to |
| up |

Complete each of the gaps with one of the words from the box.

1 The neighbours had a party last night and we didn't **get** _______ **sleep** till about 3.
2 I **stayed** _______ to watch the boxing last night – it started just after midnight.
3 Our daughter still doesn't **sleep** _______ **the night** – she always wakes up at least once.
4 She went to bed exhausted and immediately **fell** _______ **a deep sleep**.
5 The review of his performance was far from complimentary, but he wasn't going to **lose any sleep** _______ **it**.
6 I'm going to **sleep** _______ **it** tonight and I'll let you know my decision tomorrow.
7 I couldn't tell you what happened – I **nodded** _______ just before the end of the film.
8 A surprisingly high percentage of the population **suffers** _______ **insomnia**.

### B Abilities

Match each sentence beginning **1–6** with an appropriate ending **a–f**.

1 This highly talented artist has **an eye**
2 Realizing he did not have **a good ear**
3 The young reporter clearly had **a nose**
4 He admits that he doesn't have **a head**
5 Dave did it himself; he is **a dab hand**
6 Being bilingual he has **a natural flair**

a **for figures**, and he leaves all the accounting work to his wife, Pam.
b **for music**, he gave up trying to learn the piano and took up acting instead.
c **for languages**, and has taught himself Russian, Greek and Polish.
d **for detail** and many of his works are mistaken for photographs.
e **for a good story** and he wrote several exclusives for the popular tabloid.
f **at DIY** and wouldn't dream of getting a builder in to do anything.

### Self help

Study the expressions in bold in B for one minute. Then cover the sentence endings a–f and look only at the beginnings 1–6. How many expressions can you remember?

### C Adjectives in film reviews

Match each of the adjectives to an appropriate description.

| | | | |
|---|---|---|---|
| moving | gripping | stunning | innovative |
| clichéd | over-hyped | excruciating | unconvincing |

1 Both the plot and the characters were difficult to believe. _______________
2 It contains some very new and original animation techniques. _______________
3 We've seen this type of thing so many times before. _______________
4 It had me on the edge of my seat. _______________
5 It didn't live up to the expectations created by all the publicity. _______________
6 Take a big box of tissues to this one – you'll need them. _______________
7 Painful to watch; the most boring film of the year. _______________
8 She gave an amazing performance – her most impressive yet. _______________

## Language focus

Grammar reference on page 220 of the Coursebook.

1 In **1–5** below, decide which sentence, **a** or **b**, follows on more naturally from the first sentence.

**1** Captain John Simms, the controversial chairman of league leaders Greendale United, is in the news again.

**a** The 59-year-old former ex-Army officer **has announced** his intention to cut players' wages by 10% if they fail to win their semi-final cup match against neighbours Bromwich City on Saturday.

**b** The intention to cut players' wages by 10% if they fail to win their semi-final cup match against neighbours Bromwich City on Saturday **has been announced** by the 59-year-old ex-Army officer.

**2** After Paris, this magnificent collection of paintings moves to the Reina Sofia Museum in Madrid, where it will remain until January.

**a** A number of leading financial organizations, including two major Spanish banks and the French insurance giant ULP, which devotes 1% of its profits to the arts, **have sponsored** the exhibition.

**b** The exhibition **has been sponsored** by a number of leading financial organizations, including two major Spanish banks and the French insurance giant ULP, which devotes 1% of its profits to the arts.

**3** Annette Sawyer is the brainiest student in town!

**a** The people marking her GCSE examination papers **have awarded** the sixteen-year-old from Brayton High School top marks in all eleven of her exams, a record for any pupil from Tipton, past or present.

**b** The sixteen-year-old from Brayton High School **has been awarded** top marks in all eleven of her GCSE exams, a record for any pupil from Tipton, past or present.

**4** The driver of a delivery van is recovering in hospital from head injuries sustained in a curious incident which occurred in the centre of Worthing yesterday.

**a** Paul Roberts of Kingston Lane, Shoreham, was on his way home when he **crashed into** a lorry parked outside the main post office in Harper Street.

**b** A lorry parked outside the main post office in Harper Street **was crashed into** by Paul Roberts of Kingston Lane, Shoreham, as he was on his way home.

**5** Everything is done to ensure maximum comfort and relaxation for our guests during their stay at the Wilton Hotel.

**a** The cleaners **do not** come in to **clean** your room until 11am each day, so as not to disturb you.

**b** Rooms **are not cleaned** until 11am each day in order to avoid possible disturbance.

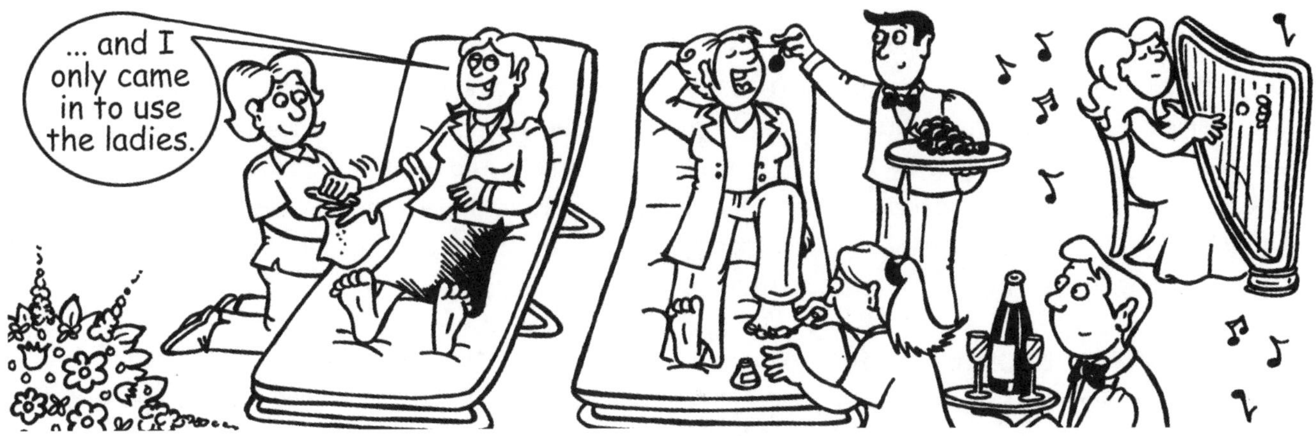


Everything is done to ensure maximum comfort and relaxation for our guests during their stay at the Wilton Hotel.

2 Complete the second sentence so that it has a similar meaning to the first sentence. There is an example at the beginning **(0)**.

**0** Everyone knows she is a close friend of the Prime Minister.
She *is known to be a close friend of the Prime Minister* .

**1** It is understood that the company is planning a takeover bid for its rival.
The company ______________________________ .

**2** Police say the offences took place on Monday.
The offences ______________________________ .

**3** It is believed that the injured motorcyclist was travelling at over 100 mph.
The injured ______________________________ .

**4** Experts thought that infected chickens were responsible for the outbreak of flu.
Infected chickens ______________________________ .

**5** They alleged she had lied in order to protect her boyfriend.
She ______________________________ .

**6** Someone stole my camera last weekend.
I had ______________________________ .

**7** Your eyes need testing.
You need ______________________________ .

**8** My foot became stuck in the hole.
I ______________________________ .

## Use of English

CAE Part 2

### Open cloze

For questions **1–15**, read the text below and think of the word which best fits each gap. Use only **one** word in each gap. There is an example at the beginning **(0)**.

#### Snoring

Sleep deprivation can make us very angry, which is **(0)** *why* snoring – the human equivalent of a car alarm **(1)** ______ set off at night – can be so irritating. Most people snore occasionally, but in middle age about 40 per cent of men and 20 per cent of women **(2)** ______ so regularly. Snoring can ruin relationships and be intensely embarrassing. Snorers **(3)** ______ go into hospital, for example, may worry that they'll keep the whole ward awake. But snoring doesn't **(4)** ______ afflict the unafflicted; snorers may also disturb **(5)** ______ and feel sleepy during the day.

Snoring can sometimes be a symptom of a more serious condition. Up **(6)** ______ six per cent of men and two per cent of women suffer from sleep apnoea, a syndrome in which breathing **(7)** ______ significantly disrupted during sleep. Some people may start off **(8)** ______ uncomplicated snorers, but develop sleep apnoea as they get older. The word apnoea is derived **(9)** ______ the Greek and means 'no breathing'. People **(10)** ______ sleep apnoea have airways that become obstructed during sleep. Typically, they snore loudly, stop breathing, struggle **(11)** ______ air, partly wake up (although often unaware of it), gulp a bit, and then recommence snoring. The cycle may **(12)** ______ repeated over 100 times an hour.

**(13)** ______ surprisingly, people with sleep apnoea feel unrefreshed in the morning. They may have problems concentrating during the day, feel depressed and fall asleep **(14)** ______ socially unacceptable times. At worst, they can fall asleep **(15)** ______ driving or operating dangerous machinery.

CAE Part 3

## Word formation

For questions **1–10** use the word given in capitals at the end of some of the lines to form a word that fits in the gap **in the same line**. There is an example at the beginning **(0)**.

### Genetic genius

According to a recent study the best **(0)** *musicians* are born, not made. **MUSIC**
**(1)** __________ at St Thomas's Hospital in London claim that genes are **RESEARCH**
responsible for up to 80 per cent of our ability to recognize pitch, the key
to musical **(2)** __________ . The discovery by the hospital's Twin Research **GREAT**
Unit, the largest of its kind in the world, accounts for the prevalence of musical
families from the Bachs to the Corrs and the Strausses to the Jacksons. In a
'distorted tunes test' over 500 twins were played a **(3)** __________ of popular **VARY**
songs, each **(4)** __________ a number of errors. A comparison of the **CONTAIN**
**(5)** __________ of identical twins with those of non-identical twins revealed **RESPOND**
that the former were **(6)** __________ better at spotting the mistakes. The **NOTICE**
results of the study suggest that for some children, music lessons may only go
so far in improving musical abilities such as pitch **(7)** __________. However, **RECOGNIZE**
parents hoping to save money on lessons cannot use the test as an early
indicator of musical potential: it is **(8)** __________ for children under 12, who **RELY**
do not have sufficient **(9)** __________ of the tunes played. For its next project, **KNOW**
the Twin Research Unit will test whether identical twins can tell us if genes have
a role to play in a **(10)** __________ for classical, jazz or pop music. **PREFER**

# Writing

CAE Part 2

## Article

1 Read the following Writing Part 2 task and the two versions of the same article below. Which of the versions is more likely to be published? Give reasons for your answer.

You see the announcement below in *Live and Learn*, an international magazine.

> ***The best days of your life?***
>
> We invite you, our readers, to submit an article on the secondary school you used to attend or are attending now.
>
> We'd like you to:
>
> - tell us about the positive and negative aspects of your secondary school
> - give your overall opinion of the education you received or are receiving
> - say how typical the school was or is of other schools in your country.
>
> We will publish the most interesting article from each country.

Write your **article** in **220–260** words.

**Version A**

## My school

In my secondary school the teachers were very strict and they did not allow us to talk at all during the lessons. They used boring teaching methods like dictation, and they were not very friendly towards the pupils.

To show how superior they were, the teachers always addressed us by our surname and many wore the traditional cap and gown in class. They thought that they had all the knowledge and we would learn just by listening to them. They were all men; there were no women teachers in our school. Other schools in the country had a more progressive type of education, the students did more in lessons and there were mixed ability classes. My school and a few others like it still had passive learning and iron discipline.

However, students got good marks, except the ones who did not behave well. There were a lot of students who were good at sport and the sports facilities were very good. We had a swimming pool and squash courts, and a language laboratory and some video recorders. Every year some of the rich students went to Interlaken in Switzerland.

But I don't think my school prepared me very well for the world of work. I also think the education wasn't general enough and it didn't teach me to think for myself.

**Version B**

## *Distance learning: formal address in formal dress*

*"Cease this idle chatter, boys; there will be no talking. I shall dictate and you will write." This was an all too common instruction at the secondary school I had the misfortune to attend, and helps to illustrate the teaching methods used and the distance that teachers liked to keep from their pupils.*

*They always addressed us by our surname and, as if to demonstrate their superiority further, many would regularly wear the traditional cap and gown in class. The teacher was the source of all knowledge, and his students – this was an all-male institution – merely empty vessels to be filled. Whilst the trend up and down the country was towards a more progressive type of education, with greater student involvement and mixed ability classes, my own school and a few others like it, seemed trapped in a time bubble of passive learning and iron discipline.*

*Having said all that, I cannot deny that academic achievement was high, provided, of course, you didn't rebel against the system. And the school's many talented young sportsmen were able to make use of its extensive sports facilities. Indeed, unlike most other schools at the time, ours boasted a swimming pool and squash courts, as well as a language laboratory and a number of video recorders. There was even an annual trip to Interlaken in Switzerland – for those whose parents could afford it.*

*But how many of us can say we were adequately prepared for the world of work which awaited us? How many of us can claim we ended our schooldays as fully rounded individuals capable of thinking for ourselves? I'm not sure I can.*

2 Identify the part or parts of **Version B** in which each of the following are mentioned:

**a** the positive aspects of the school
**b** the negative aspects of the school
**c** his overall opinion of the education he received
**d** how typical the school was of others in his country.

3 Write your own answer to the question. Before you do, complete the exercises in **A** and **B** below.

**A Planning**

**1** When planning your answer you might consider some of the following main categories:

| | | | |
|---|---|---|---|
| Facilities | Teachers | Academic achievement | Extra-curricular activities |
| Discipline | Teaching and learning methods | | Range of subjects |

In **1–7**, match each of the main categories to the related ideas. The first one has been done for you.

| **Main categories** | **Related ideas** |
|---|---|
| **1** Teachers: | knowledge, skills, ability to motivate, empathy |
| **2** ______: | theoretical or practical, variety, student involvement, interest |
| **3** ______: | types of punishment and their effectiveness |
| **4** ______: | wide or limited, broad education or specialization |
| **5** ______: | exam results, school's 'success' |
| **6** ______: | buildings, equipment eg computers, laboratories etc |
| **7** ______: | clubs, societies, sporting activities, excursions, holidays |

**2** Which of these categories are mentioned in **Version B**?

**B Beginnings and endings**

**1** What techniques are used to begin and end **Version B**?

**2** Match each of the article beginnings **1–5** with a technique in the box.

| | | |
|---|---|---|
| An unusual statement | A fact or statistic | A question |
| A story | A comparison | |

**1** According to recent figures, there is a computer for every six secondary school pupils in this country. Clearly, those who compiled these figures did not visit my school, where there are over a thousand pupils and no more than a dozen computers.

**2** Have you ever wondered how different your life might have been if you'd gone to a different school? I know I have, and it makes me realize just how fortunate I was to attend St Cuthbert's comprehensive in Pencaster.

**3** A terrified young boy walks into the headmaster's office and receives six strokes of the cane – as punishment for talking in class. Ten years later the same boy, a young man now, walks into the courtroom and receives a 15-year prison sentence – as punishment for a vicious assault. I wonder how many more violent criminals were the product of brutal regimes at school.

**4** There's nothing like a gentle ear massage and a short session of air writing with your nose to refresh the mind before a session on geometry. 'Brain breaks' such as these were an integral part of my schooling and I cannot speak highly enough of them.

**5** You wouldn't ask an ex-convict if he enjoyed his spell in jail. And you probably wouldn't ask a recently discharged patient whether she had a good time in hospital. So please don't ask me if I enjoyed my 7 years at Hove County Grammar School for Boys!

**Don't forget!**

- Plan your answer using the ideas in 3 A above.
- Engage the reader's interest in the first paragraph using one of the techniques in 3 B above.
- End the article in an interesting or thought-provoking way.
- Use a range of vocabulary and structures.
- Give your article a title which reflects the content of the article.

Now you are ready to write your article.

# 7 Feeling good

## Reading

CAE Part 2

### Gapped text

1 You are going to read an extract from a magazine article. Six paragraphs have been removed from the extract. Choose from the paragraphs **A–G** on page 53 the one which fits each gap **(1–6)**. There is one extra paragraph which you do not need to use.

## The boy who broke every rule in the book

*Was Nicholas Culpeper a medical rebel who challenged the establishment, or simply a quack*, asks Scarlett Thomas.*

Anyone who has ever used peppermint tea to ease indigestion or taken chamomile for a good night's sleep has been using herbal medicine. However suspicious some of us may be of a complete system of 'alternative' healing, we all know that, for example, vinegar is good on wasp stings, and honey helps a sore throat.

| 1 | |
|---|---|

These are questions which have persisted for centuries. Who has the right to medical knowledge? And how could you make sure you were in safe hands? It is to the 16th century, with its complex medical system of quacks, midwives, apothecaries and a few physicians, that Benjamin Woolley first takes us in his book *The Herbalist.* We learn of Henry VIII's answer to the problem of national regulation: the creation of the *College of Physicians*, the members of which were given licensing and fining powers – but not the power to dispense medicines, which was instead held by the apothecaries, the pharmacists of the time.

| 2 | |
|---|---|

Although they were supposed to practise only in accordance with the *Pharmacopoeia Londinensis*, a huge book of instructions and recipes created by the *College of Physicians*, most apothecaries did not actually read Latin. This inability meant that they could not in fact read the book.

| 3 | |
|---|---|

Even without Latin, most apothecaries had some idea of what their medicines did. And despite not understanding the Latin slurs on their characters in the *Pharmacopoeia*, the apothecaries also knew that the College had it in for them. In 1634, Nicholas Culpeper, aged 18, arrived in London with £50 in his pocket, looking for an apprenticeship. He soon became an apprentice to an apothecary, becoming familiar with long lists of 'simple' ingredients set out in the *Pharmacopoeia*, including bizarre items like human blood and earthworms.

| 4 | |
|---|---|

So eventually abandoning his apprenticeship and despite all the rules created by the *College of Physicians*, Culpeper set up on his own as an 'independent', trading out of a shop in London's Threadneedle Street. His aim was to provide medical help for anyone who needed it and to treat people with simply prepared, locally sourced medicines. This career was interrupted by a stint as a soldier in the Civil War. It was shortly after it ended in 1649 that there was a widespread call for all legal matters to be conducted in English, so justice could be heard and understood by all.

| 5 | |
|---|---|

When it appeared, it was twice as long as the original, bulging with additions and corrections. It also explained what the recipes were for. 'In translating the book,' Woolley notes, 'Nicholas broke every rule in it.' This was seen not just as a medical act but a deeply political one. *The College of Physicians* was outraged.

| 6 | |
|---|---|

Was Culpeper a quack? No more so than the medical establishment of the time, argues Woolley. It was the *College's Pharmacopoeia* after all that recommended the use of the treatments based on ground gall stones of Persian goats that surely led to King Charles II's death. Yet Culpeper's legacy – the idea that medicine is not something that should be controlled by the elite but something belonging to everybody – is as important now as it was in the 17th century.

**a quack – a negative term to describe someone who pretends to possess medical knowledge and acts as a doctor*

A Perhaps this was fortunate, as the book warned of 'the deceit of those people who are allowed to sell the most filthy concoctions, and even mud, under the name and title of medicaments for the sake of profit'. This was undoubtedly an attack on the capabilities and moral principles of the apothecaries.

B As odd as these may seem, many recipes would also call for the drug opium, which at the time, cost less than garden rhubarb. Culpeper did not have a good experience at this time, being assigned a new master on several occasions. Then again, this was probably not a good time for anyone to be in his position, when rules meant you could be summoned to a company 'court' for having 'stubbornness and long hair'.

C *The English Physician*, Culpeper's later book, better known as *Culpeper's Complete Herbal*, did little to pacify them. It outlined not only the uses of healing plants but also Culpeper's holistic view of medicine. Despite upsetting the establishment, it became one of the most popular and enduring books in British history.

D When things get more serious, of course, most people rush to the doctor. But what if the doctor gets it wrong? Or imagine a situation when, for whatever reasons, you wanted to find out how to use other plants to heal yourself.

E Mutual distrust and rivalry between these groups seem to have defined the medical system of the next 100 years. It wasn't until the great plague that things were shaken up. London was left almost empty of doctors, with only apothecaries still providing medical care.

F It reveals a profound insight into the trade practices of the time, and how the establishment view of who should be allowed to trade and under what conditions affected everything. This was especially true concerning the health of people denied control over their medical treatment.

G Impressed by this, Culpeper's thoughts turned to a similar democratisation of medical texts. These thoughts would be made reality when he was commissioned to produce an English edition of the *Pharmacopoeia*.

2 Look at these two sentences from the text. What is the meaning of the phrasal verbs in bold?

[Culpeper became] familiar with long lists of 'simple' ingredients ***set out*** in the *Pharmacopoeia*.

[He] ***set up*** on his own as an 'independent', trading out of a shop in London's Threadneedle Street.

3 Match each of the phrasal verbs in sentences **1–7** with an appropriate definition **a–g**.

***Example:*** 1 c

**1** Let's stay at home – it looks as though the rain's **set in** for the day.
**2** I put on my old clothes and **set about** clearing out the garden shed.
**3** You should aim to **set aside** at least 15 minutes each day for physical exercise.
**4** Strike action **set back** the building of the Olympic stadium by several weeks.
**5** We **set off** at 6 in the morning and got there just before midday.
**6** It is the quality of her writing which **sets** her **apart** from other children's authors.
**7** No sooner had he jumped down into the garden than he was **set upon** by two enormous guard dogs.

**a** delay the progress of something
**b** start doing something
**c** start and seem likely to continue
**d** attack somebody
**e** reserve time for a specific purpose
**f** make somebody different from others
**g** start a journey

## Vocabulary

Wordlist on page 213 of the Coursebook.

### Phrasal verbs

Complete each gap with the appropriate form of one of the verbs from the box. In each section, **1–6**, the verb required for both gaps, **a** and **b**, is the same. There is an example at the beginning **(0)**.

| | | | |
|---|---|---|---|
| wear | put | ~~pass~~ | break |
| come | get | bring | |

**0 a** He _passed_ **out** at the sight of blood, and didn't regain consciousness for over a minute.

**b** She should have taken the day off work – she _passed_ her cold **on** to everyone in the office.

**1 a** He suffered a heart attack, which may have been ________ **on** by stress.

**b** She was unconscious, so I ________ her **round** by throwing water over her face.

**2 a** My energy levels are low, and I feel absolutely ________ **out** when I get home from work.

**b** Soon after the effects of the drug had ________ **off**, she felt an acute pain in her stomach.

**3 a** I know I ought to go to the dentist's, but I never seem to ________ **round to** making an appointment.

**b** I hope I ________ **over** this flu soon – I don't want to be ill when I go on holiday.

**4 a** The cholera epidemic ________ **out** in Peru in January 1991 and spread rapidly to neighbouring countries.

**b** I'm allergic to dairy products; the last time I ate a yoghurt, I ________ **out in** a nasty rash.

**5 a** I'm in agony – I tried to lift up the television on my own and I ________ my back **out**.

**b** She was suffering from an upset stomach, which she ________ **down to** the fish she'd eaten the night before.

**6 a** Denise has just phoned from her sick bed – she's ________ **down with** a flu bug, apparently.

**b** Scientists have yet to ______ **up with** the definitive cure for baldness.

### Word formation

1 Complete the table with the infinitives of the verbs formed from the words in the box. The first two have been done for you.

| | | | | | |
|---|---|---|---|---|---|
| ~~sure~~ | ~~strong~~ | courage | deaf | high | danger |
| deep | rich | broad | sad | force | |

| -en | en- |
|---|---|
| *strengthen* | *ensure* |

2 Complete each of the gaps using the appropriate form of the word in capitals at the end of the line. There is an example at the beginning **(0)**.

| | |
|---|---|
| **0** In an effort to *ensure* **success** in next year's European competition, | **SURE** |
| United have *strengthened* their **team** by buying two outstanding overseas players. | **STRONG** |
| **1** The build-up of troops in the border area has ___________ **tension** between the two countries. | **HIGH** |
| **2** Faced with a rapidly ___________ economic **crisis**, the Prime Minister was coming under increasing pressure to resign. | **DEEP** |
| **3** Despite rocketing unemployment figures, the President insisted that there were some ___________ **signs** of recovery in the economy. | **COURAGE** |
| **4** Join the World Wildlife Fund and help protect ___________ **species** from extinction. | **DANGER** |
| **5** The FBI is perhaps the best known of America's **law** ___________ **agencies**. | **FORCE** |
| **6** She was **deeply** ___________ by the death of her cat. | **SAD** |
| **7** There is no doubt that the school's work experience programme ___________ | **BROAD** |
| **the outlook** of its pupils and greatly ___________ **their lives**. | **RICH** |
| **8** His audience found the joke offensive and greeted it with a ___________ **silence**. | **DEAF** |

## Self help

Add the collocations in bold in exercise 2 to your vocabulary notebook.

# Language focus

Grammar reference on page 221 of the Coursebook.

## Reported speech

1 Cross out the two options which **cannot** be used to complete each sentence. There is an example at the beginning **(0)**.

**0** The doctor *reassured*/~~*explained*~~/*promised*/~~*mentioned*~~ her that the drugs would have no serious side-effects.

**1** She *invited/refused/offered/asked* me to go on holiday with her.

**2** David *denied/admitted/confessed/claimed* to being a little nervous before the operation.

**3** We were *accused/blamed/told off/complained* for causing the disruption.

**4** My mother *persuaded/encouraged/insisted/requested* I go with her to the hospital.

**5** Several people have *commented/complimented/remarked/congratulated* on Sally's new look.

**6** Zoe's beautician *advised/suggested/argued/warned* her against having cosmetic surgery.

**7** We tried to *dissuade/discourage/urge/convince* her from going through with it, as well.

**8** It has been *told/assured/announced/confirmed* that the security forces will be on maximum alert.

**9** My boss could see I was stressed out and he *advised/suggested/proposed/recommended* me to take a few days' holiday.

**10** She found a dead spider in her salad and *demanded/ordered/asked/insisted* to see the manager.

2 Rewrite each sentence in two different ways. In each gap you should write **between two and four words**. There is an example at the beginning **(0)**.

**0** 'I'll help you do your homework later,' she told him.

**a** She said that *she would help him* do his homework later.

**b** She promised *to help him* do his homework later.

**1** 'I'll cut you out of my will if you marry George,' he told his daughter.

**a** He said that ______________ his daughter out of his will if she married George.

**b** He threatened ______________ his daughter out of his will if she married George.

**2** 'I think you should take a few days off work,' he told me.

**a** He said he ______________ a few days off work.

**b** He suggested ______________ a few days off work.

**3** 'You must leave immediately!' she told them.

**a** She said that ______________ immediately.

**b** She ordered ______________ immediately.

**4** 'I've always loved you,' he told her.

**a** He said that ______________ her.

**b** He confessed to ______________ her.

**5** 'It wasn't me who stole it,' she insisted.

**a** She insisted that she ______________ .

**b** She denied ______________ .

**6** There's a rumour that they paid her over $3 million for her part in the film.

**a** It is rumoured that she ______________ over $3 million for her part in the film.

**b** She is rumoured ______________ over $3 million for her part in the film.

**7** 'Can you take my name off the list?' he asked her.

**a** He asked her if ______________ his name off the list.

**b** He requested that ______________ be included on the list.

**8** 'Aliens abducted me,' he told journalists.

**a** He assured journalists that he ______________ by aliens.

**b** He claimed to ______________ by aliens.

'It wasn't me who stole it,' she insisted.

# Use of English

CAE Part 1

## Multiple-choice cloze

For questions **1–12**, read the text below and decide which answer **(A, B, C** or **D)** best fits each gap. There is an example at the beginning **(0)**.

### The new way to burn fat

People who want to lose weight are being **(0)** _____ a startling new way to burn fat. Would-be slimmers are flocking to a spa in Hong Kong that **(1)** _____ to reduce their waistlines by smearing them with Chinese herbs, dousing them with alcohol and then **(2)** _____ light to them, all for £78 a session. The spa claims that the **(3)** _____ heat of the fire penetrates deep tissue, increasing circulation and helping the body to absorb the herbal concoction which works to detoxify the body and **(4)** _____ down fat. It boasts that the results are **(5)** _____ , with customers recording losses of up to 15 centimetres of fat after the first session.

Karen Chu, owner of The Life of Life Healing Spa in Hong Kong's busy Causeway Bay district, says that about 100 customers have successfully **(6)** _____ the treatment, and there have been no **(7)** _____. 'About half the customers come here for the Aqua-Fire treatment,' she said. 'It is **(8)** _____ safe. You are **(9)** _____ from the flame by wet towels. We have never had any complaints or problems. In Asia, people are more **(10)** _____ to the idea of fire being a healing treatment. It is only the Westerners who are afraid of the fire. If a customer is really afraid we don't go **(11)** _____.' Ms Chu claims the fire treatment also boosts the immune system, relieves stress, cleanses the skin and **(12)** _____ muscular pains and stomach problems.

| | A | B | C | D |
|---|---|---|---|---|
| **0** | proposed | suggested | offered | advanced |
| **1** | predicts | promises | considers | assures |
| **2** | making | giving | holding | setting |
| **3** | soaking | bitter | intense | forced |
| **4** | bring | take | work | break |
| **5** | immediate | early | straight | rushed |
| **6** | undercut | undergone | underused | undertaken |
| **7** | casualties | damages | warnings | cautions |
| **8** | strongly | fiercely | perfectly | deeply |
| **9** | prevented | kept | protected | stopped |
| **10** | familiar | acceptable | prepared | open |
| **11** | through | ahead | forward | along |
| **12** | eases | disappears | lightens | recovers |

CAE Part 2

## Open cloze

For questions **1–15**, read the text below and think of the word that best fits each gap. Use only one word in each gap. There is an example at the beginning. **(0)**

### It's Easy to Work Out

Many people exercise **(0)** _with_ the aim of achieving a flat tummy but it isn't necessary to contort your body painfully to **(1)** _______ so. Both yoga and Pilates **(2)** _______ known to build amazing abdominal strength and give you greater awareness **(3)** _______ your pelvic floor muscles. It is **(4)** _______ muscles, once strengthened, that will provide greater support **(5)** _______ vulnerable backs.

Doing crunches is one of the best ways to flatten your tummy. **(6)** _______ involves first lying on the floor, with your hands **(7)** _______ side of your head. Raise your head approximately fifteen centimetres off the ground, then pause in this position for five seconds **(8)** _______ lowering it back down. You should also bend your legs, raise them and cross your ankles while doing the crunches so **(9)** _______ to ensure that your stomach muscles do the work, **(10)** _______ your back. **(11)** _______ you do have back problems, using a Swiss ball when you're exercising will help protect it, too. You can place it between you and a wall, for example, and roll down it **(12)** _______ you reach a squatting position. It's also fun to try to balance on one while you're lifting weights because not **(13)** _______ are the muscles in your arms **(14)** _______ used but your abdomen will be working hard to keep **(15)** _______ from falling off.

## Writing

CAE Part 2

### Review

1 Read the following Writing Part 2 task.

The magazine published by your English club has asked its readers to send in a review of a film or book which includes a sporting theme. Write a review for the magazine commenting on the importance of the sporting theme in the film or book and saying how well you think it is handled. You should also say why you think others might or might not enjoy seeing the film or reading the book.

2 Read the following answer, ignoring the gaps for the moment. Does the review address all parts of the task?

# 'Ali' 10 years in the life of Muhammad Ali

**'I AM THE GREATEST!'** exclaims Will Smith in the **(1)** _________ role of this compelling film about the former world heavyweight boxing champion. But these words apply equally well to Smith's own extremely powerful acting **(2)** _________ as the man who was named sportsperson of the century in several countries including his own. Smith looks, moves and talks like the legendary boxer, and his well-deserved Oscar **(3)** _________ for Best Actor is reason enough to see the film.

Boxing is clearly central to the film, which is **(4)** _________ in the period from Ali's title-winning defeat of Sonny Liston in 1964 to his regaining of the crown from George Foreman a decade later. To the untrained eye, the boxing **(5)** _________ are entirely convincing, and succeed in conveying both the passion and the horror of the sport. The film builds up to a dramatic **(6)** _________ with the 1974 fight in Zaire, and the combination of Michael Mann's expert direction and the moving musical **(7)** _________ makes this one of the most memorable moments of the film.

But don't be put off if you're not a boxing fan – the film is as much about the social context in which the **(8)** _________ takes place as about heavyweight fights. It provides a fascinating **(9)** _________ into nineteen sixties America and Ali's response to contemporary attitudes. It explores his relationship with the black Muslims and also shows how he risked his career and his freedom by refusing induction into the army at the time of the Vietnam War.

There's something for everyone in the film: sport, history, drama, romance and even humour. Many of the boxer's witty **(10)** _________ , particularly those delivered to journalists, will have you laughing out loud and developing an affection for one of the world's truly great sporting heroes.

3 Complete each of the gaps with one of the words from the box.

| | | | |
|---|---|---|---|
| scenes | lines | insight | action |
| performance | set | title | nomination |
| climax | score | | |

4 Underline those adjectives used by the writer to express an opinion on the film or the acting. Underline any accompanying adverbs or nouns.

***Example**: compelling film*

5 What other expressions are used by the writer to encourage readers to see the film?

6 Either: **a** write your own answer to the task in exercise 1
or: **b** answer the following question:

The magazine published by your English club has asked its readers to send in a review of a film or book whose content is largely biographical. Write a review for the magazine commenting on what you learnt from the film or book and saying why you think others might or might not enjoy it.

Write your **review** in **220–260** words.

## Don't forget!

- **Do not** write a long summary of the film or book.
- **Do** express your opinion throughout the review.

## Before you write

In the Coursebook read page 76 in Unit 6 and page 203 in Ready for Writing.

# 8 This is the modern world

## Reading

CAE Part 3

### Multiple choice

1 You are going to read a magazine article. For questions **1–7**, choose the answer **(A**, **B**, **C** or **D)** which you think fits best according to the text.

## The truth is out there on the net

*Far from encouraging mass deceit, the web promotes honesty because we fear getting caught, writes Clive Thompson.*

Everyone tells a little white lie now and then but Cornell University professor, Jeffrey Hancock, recently claimed to have established the truth of a curious proposition: we fib less frequently when we're online than when talking in person. He asked thirty undergraduates to record all their communications, and all their lies for a week. When he tallied the results, he found the students had mishandled the truth in about one-quarter of all face-to-face conversations, and in a whopping 37 per cent of phone calls. But when they went into cyberspace, only 1 in 5 instant-messaging chats contained a lie, and barely 14 per cent of email messages were dishonest. Obviously, you can't make generalisations about society solely on the basis of college students' behaviour, and there's also something odd about asking people to be honest about how often they lie. But still, Professor Hancock's results were intriguing, not least because they upend some of our primary expectations about life on the net.

Wasn't cyberspace supposed to be the scary zone where you couldn't trust anyone? Back when the Internet first went mainstream, those pundits in the government, media and academia worried that the digital age would open the floodgates of deception. Since anyone could hide behind an anonymous hotmail address or chat-room nickname, net users, we were warned, would be free to lie with impunity. Parents panicked and frantically supervised their children's use of cyberspace, under the assumption that anyone lurking out there in the unknown was a threat until proved otherwise. And to a certain extent, you can see their reasoning: if we go along with the basic introduction to any psychology course, we're more likely to lie to people when there's distance between us. Eventually, though, many suspicions turned out to be unfounded.

What is it, then, about online life that makes us more truthful? It's simple: we're worried about being exposed. In 'real' life, after all, it's pretty easy to get away with deception. If you lie to someone at a party, you can always claim you said no such thing. On the Internet, your words often come back to haunt you. The digital age is tough on liars, as an endless parade of executives are finding out. This isn't a problem for only corporate barons. We read the headlines; we know in cyberspace our words never die, because machines don't forget. "It's a cut-and-paste culture," as Professor Hancock put it, though he said that on the phone, so who knows if he really meant it? And consider that many email programs automatically 'quote' your words when someone replies to your message. Every time I finish an email message, I pause for a few seconds to reread it just to ensure I haven't said something I'll later regret.

Maybe this helps explain why television programmes like *CSI: Crime Scene Investigation* have become so popular. They're all about revealing the sneaky things that people do. We watch with fascination and unease as scientists inspect the tiniest of clues – a stray hair on a car seat, a latent fingerprint on a CD-ROM. After you've seen high-tech cops rake over evidence from a crime scene with ultraviolet light and luminal and genetic sequencers enough times, you get the message: Watch out – we've got files on you. Forensic science has become the central drama of pop culture, and our fascination with it may well add to our anxieties about technology. So no wonder we're so careful to restrict our lying to low-technology environments. We have begun to be keenly suspicious of places that might be bugged, conducting all of our subterfuge in loud restaurants and lonely parks.

Still, it's not only the fear of electronic exposure that drives us to tell the truth. There's something about the Internet that encourages us to 'tell all', often in rather outrageous ways. Psychologists have noticed for years that going online seems to have a catalytic effect on people's personalities. The most quiet and reserved people may become deranged loudmouths when they sit behind the keyboard. Others stay up until dawn and conduct angry debates on discussion boards with total strangers. You can usually spot the newcomers in any discussion group because they're the ones WRITING IN CAPITALS – they're overwhelmed by the Internet's heady combination of geographic distance and pseudo-invisibility.

Our impulse to confess via cyberspace inverts much of what we think about honesty. It used to be if you wanted to really trust someone, you arranged a face-to-face meeting. Our culture still obsesses over physical contact, the shaking of hands, the lubricating chitchat. Executives and politicians spend hours flying across the country merely for a five-minute meeting, on the assumption that even a few seconds of face time can cut through the prevarications of letters and legal contracts. But perhaps this growing tendency towards online communication is gratifying news. We could find ourselves living in an increasingly honest world. It will at least, inevitably, be one in which there are increasingly severe penalties for deception. With its unforgiving machine memory, the Internet might turn out to be the unlikely conscience of the world.

**1** What does the writer suggest about Professor Hancock's findings?
**A** They prove a higher than average level of dishonesty amongst students.
**B** They are unreliable as students are not likely to have kept accurate records.
**C** They only demonstrate what was already common knowledge to most people.
**D** Students are less likely to lie while chatting online than on the telephone.

**2** What does the writer state about the early days of Internet use?
**A** There was no discernible change in the general level of honest behaviour.
**B** The Internet provided people with new ways to commit crime.
**C** Children were frequently not permitted any kind of access to the Internet.
**D** There was some over-reaction to the perceived dangers of the Internet.

**3** What point is illustrated by the references to email records?
**A** The corporate world has been forced to reassess its systems of communication.
**B** People have developed a less trusting attitude towards others they deal with.
**C** People are becoming more cautious with regard to the content of email.
**D** Email and similar documentation has sometimes been used to manipulate the truth.

**4** According to the writer, television programmes on forensic science have
**A** led to people becoming more frightened of being exposed.
**B** encouraged people to adopt more sophisticated methods of deception.
**C** overtaken other types of television drama in terms of popularity.
**D** given people a false impression of what science can currently achieve.

**5** In the fifth paragraph, what are we told about the effect of Internet chatrooms on people?
**A** They have had a beneficial influence on some naturally shy people.
**B** They have allowed certain people to express themselves more concisely.
**C** They have led to a transformation in some people's usual behaviour.
**D** They have improved relations between people from different cultures.

**6** What does the writer state about the future impact of online communication?
**A** People will ensure that emails are strictly accurate and honest.
**B** Instances of dishonesty will have more serious consequences.
**C** People will feel the need for legal advice when preparing certain documents.
**D** It will remove the need for face-to-face contact.

**7** In these paragraphs, the writer is
**A** commenting on the varied uses of the Internet.
**B** complaining about a lack of online security.
**C** expressing doubt about the benefits of computers.
**D** explaining an unexpected side-effect of modern technology.

2 Underline the following words and expressions **1–3** in the first paragraph of the text, then match each one to its definition **a–c**.

| | |
|---|---|
| **1** tell a white lie | **a** an informal word meaning *to lie* |
| **2** fib | **b** a euphemism for *to lie* |
| **3** mishandle the truth | **c** to lie so as not to hurt someone's feelings |

3 In **1–5** decide whether the words in bold refer to being honest (H) or dishonest (D). There is an example at the beginning **(0)**.

**0** The Minister for Education said that the newspaper's false accusations were part of a **dirty tricks campaign** designed to harm her reputation. *D*

**1** It was a remarkably **candid confession** for a politician not normally known for his readiness to own up to his mistakes.

**2** The Prime Minister accused his deputy of employing **underhand tactics** to gain control of the party by secretly encouraging other members to vote against him.

**3** Just give me a **straight answer** to a straight question: do you intend to take the exam or not?

**4** We want the advertisement to convey the message that we are a **reputable firm** of estate agents that people can trust.

**5** Hobson's **devious plan** to blackmail blameless businessmen earned him the respect of the criminal underworld.

4 Which of the adjectives in bold in **1–5** of exercise 3 above means the following:

**a** dishonest and secretive
**b** dishonest and clever
**c** honest and reliable
**d** honest and open, especially about something difficult or painful
**e** honest and direct

**Self help**

Add the collocations in bold from exercise 3 to your vocabulary notebook.

## Vocabulary

Wordlist on page 213 of the Coursebook.

### Verbs formed with *up, down, over* and *under*

1 In **1–5** below, one of the four verbs is not a real word. Cross out the verb which does not exist.

| | | | |
|---|---|---|---|
| **1** uproot | upgrade | uphear | update |
| **2** overthrow | overgo | overrule | overhear |
| **3** undercut | undertake | underroot | undergo |
| **4** upset | uphold | upstage | uprule |
| **5** downhold | downsize | downplay | download |

2 Complete each of the gaps with one of the verbs from exercise 1. There may be more than one possible answer.

***Example:*** Rebels tried to ___overthrow___ the government.

**1** A higher court can ______________ a judge's decision.
**2** A patient may have to ______________ an operation.
**3** Computer users can regularly ______________ their existing software.
**4** A company may ______________ its competitors' prices.
**5** Governments sometimes ______________ the seriousness of a situation.

## Adjectives formed with *in, off, on, out* and *over*

Underline the correct alternative.

**1** She was momentarily blinded by the headlights of an *incoming/oncoming* **car**.

**2** These research findings represent an important contribution to the *ongoing/outgoing* **debate** on the effects of passive smoking.

**3** Only 30% of the pupils at this school actually live in the town itself; most children come in by bus from *outdoor/outlying* **areas**.

**4** First to arrive on the scene was an *off-duty/off-hand* **police officer**, who had heard the explosion from his kitchen.

**5** According to some scientists, humans have only two *inborn/overnight* **fears** – fear of falling and fear of loud noises. All others, it seems, are learned.

### Self help

Add the adjective + noun collocations in bold in the above exercise to your vocabulary notebook.

## Plans

1 The following adjectives and verbs are all collocates of the nouns ***plan*** or ***plans***. One of the items in each group is very different in meaning to the other three. Underline the odd one out.

***Example:***

| | | | |
|---|---|---|---|
| *workable* | *viable* | *controversial* (underlined) | *feasible* |

*A controversial plan is one which causes public disagreement or disapproval; the other three adjectives are used to describe plans which are likely to succeed.*

| | | | |
|---|---|---|---|
| **1** emergency | bold | daring | audacious |
| **2** elaborate | detailed | intricate | devious |
| **3** clever | ingenious | impracticable | brilliant |
| **4** draw up | devise | carry out | conceive |
| **5** scrap | abandon | jettison | put forward |
| **6** shelve | announce | unveil | reveal |

2 Complete the gaps with one of the collocates you have underlined in exercise 1 above. If the word required is a verb, write the correct form.

***Example:***
Fearing they would lose votes over the issue, the government scrapped their controversial plan to reintroduce military service.

**1** The proposed peace plan is ill-conceived and ________ : it simply will not work.

**2** Local authorities have sensibly drawn up ________ plans to be adopted in the event of further flooding.

**3** It's a brilliant plan, but rather too ________ for my liking; it might lay me open to accusations of dishonesty.

**4** Plans to build a nuclear power plant in the area have been ________ following strong public opposition.

**5** They were prevented from ________ their plan to rob the bank after a police patrol spotted their stolen car and arrested them.

**6** Management ________ a plan aimed at increasing productivity, but it was immediately rejected by union leaders.

### Self help

Add the collocates of **plan** from exercise 1 to your vocabulary notebook.

## Computer technology

1 In **A** and **B** below, combine a word on the left with a word on the right to form new items of vocabulary associated with computers or the Internet. For each new item of vocabulary decide whether it should be written as one word or two.

**A**

| | |
|---|---|
| **1** mouse | **a** top |
| **2** key | **b** cam |
| **3** lap | **c** mat |
| **4** disk | **d** board |
| **5** web | **e** drive |

**B**

| | |
|---|---|
| **1** chat | **a** engine |
| **2** home | **b** board |
| **3** search | **c** provider |
| **4** service | **d** room |
| **5** bulletin | **e** page |

2 Match each item of vocabulary you formed in exercise 1 to one of the definitions below.

**1** a portable computer
**2** camera connected to a computer so that images can be seen on the Internet
**3** an area on the Internet where a number of people can communicate with each other in real time
**4** a place on the Internet where you can read messages from others and leave your own
**5** a program used to help look for information on the Internet
**6** a piece of soft material for moving a computer mouse around on
**7** a company that provides customers with a connection to the Internet
**8** the set of keys you operate for typing or putting information into a computer
**9** part of a computer that reads information from or records information onto a disk
**10** the first web page to appear on your screen each time you log on to the Internet

# Language focus

Grammar reference on page 222 of the Coursebook.

## Talking about the future

Decide which answer **A**, **B**, **C** or **D** best fits each space.

**1** I hear that Brian and Julie are ______ to start a family soon.
**A** projecting **B** considering **C** hoping **D** assuring

**2** I ______ they'll accept the offer, but it's worth a try.
**A** suspect **B** hope **C** doubt **D** expect

**3** I'm just ______ to go out. Can I call you back later?
**A** likely **B** about **C** almost **D** soon

**4** The company has announced that all employees ______ to receive a special bonus payment at Christmas next year.
**A** arrange **B** go **C** are **D** like

**5** She's off sick today, but she may ______ be back at work tomorrow.
**A** hardly **B** probably **C** unlikely **D** well

**6** Come round at 2 o'clock – we should ______ our lunch by then.
**A** be finished **B** have to finish **C** have finished **D** have been finishing

**7** Building work is ______ to start next month, but I wouldn't be surprised if there was a delay.
**A** due **B** bound **C** willing **D** expecting

**8** No one else thinks I'll win, but I'm pretty ______ of success myself.
**A** definite **B** confident **C** assured **D** doubtless

### Determiners

In each of the following sentences there is one grammatical mistake. Correct each mistake by changing or deleting **one** of the words in bold.

***Examples:*** We aren't expecting very ~~**much**~~ *many* **more** people to turn up.
We had **a** ~~**very**~~ **lot of** problems at work today.

**1** I know of **no other any** place which is quite as beautiful as this.

**2** I try to go swimming **every another** day during the week – Mondays, Wednesdays and Fridays, usually.

**3** **Every a few** months or so we take a day off and go walking in the mountains.

**4** We only intended to spend a fortnight there, but we liked it so much we stayed for **other two** weeks.

**5** *Determined* is my favourite track on the album but there are **quite a few of** others I like as well.

**6** I've been working here for **quite some much** time – nearly ten years, in fact.

**7** There's **no much** milk left – enough for breakfast, but that's all.

**8** She's had nothing to eat for **some each three** days now – we're getting a bit worried.

## Use of English

CAE Part 2

### Open cloze

For questions **1–15**, read the text below and think of the word which best fits each gap. Use only **one** word in each gap. There is an example at the beginning **(0)**.

### Mobile phone throwing Championships

The Mobile Phone Throwing World Championships **(0)** *are* held every year in Finland, the birthplace of the first mobile phone, which was more **(1)** _____ size of a small briefcase than the tiny accessories **(2)** _____ today. When the championships first took place in 2000 there were **(3)** _____ mere 30 competitors, but now the championship attracts well **(4)** _____ 100 people from around the world, all of **(5)** _____ boiling over with frustration at one of the past century's most influential inventions.

The competition is divided **(6)** _____ two sections, contested by teams and individuals. The original category is judged simply on length of throw, but in the freestyle event competitors win on points awarded **(7)** _____ notable performances during the run-up. **(8)** _____ some competitors use their own handsets, most betray a grudging dependence on their phone **(9)** _____ selecting a missile from a large range of second-hand phones **(10)** _____ are supplied by the organizers.

The competition was founded by local business-woman Christina Lund, inspired by her observations of a country tied to **(11)** _____ mobiles. 'I saw that all of **(12)** _____ have very different emotions about our mobiles: much of the time they cause tension and frustration, especially when they get dropped. They never ring when they are supposed **(13)** _____ and they go off **(14)** _____ inconvenient times. So I had the idea of a competition based **(15)** _____ releasing some of that tension.'

CAE Part 3

## Word formation

Use the word given in capitals at the end of some of the lines to form a word that fits in the gap **in the same line**. There is an example at the beginning **(0)**.

### Obsessed with your inbox?

| | |
|---|---|
| It was not so long ago that we dealt with colleagues through face-to-face | |
| **(0)** *interaction* and with counterparts and customers by phone or | **INTERACT** |
| letter. But the world of communication has **(1)** ________ a dramatic | **GO** |
| transformation, not all for the good. Email, while **(2)** ________ a | **DOUBT** |
| swift means of communication, providing your server is fully **(3)** ________, | **FUNCTION** |
| and that the address you have contains no **(4)** ________, has had a | **ACCURATE** |
| **(5)** ________ effect on certain people's behaviour, both at home and in | **SIGNIFY** |
| business. For these people, the use of email has become **(6)** ________ | **RESIST** |
| addictive, to the extent that it is **(7)** ________ their mental and physical | **THREAT** |
| health. Addicts spend their day **(8)** ________ checking for email and | **COMPULSION** |
| have a **(9)** ________ to panic if their server goes down. It is | **TEND** |
| estimated that one in six people spend four hours a day sending and | |
| receiving messages, the equivalent to more than two working days a | |
| week. The negative effect on **(10)** ________ is something employers | **PRODUCE** |
| are well aware of. | |

CAE Part 4

## Gapped sentences

For questions **1–5** below, think of **one** word only which can be used appropriately in all three sentences. In this exercise, the words required can be found in the base text of the article *Unplugged* on page 104 of the Coursebook. Here is an example **(0)**.

**0** Alexandro's knee injury means that he may well *miss* out on the chance to play in the final.
Unless she gets here soon, she's going to *miss* the train.
A driver had a near *miss* today when a light plane made an emergency landing on a country road just ahead of him.

**1** I know that Simon meant ________ when he corrected my pronunciation, but I thought it was rude rather than helpful.
She is ________ aware of the risks involved in bungee jumping, but that's not going to stop her doing it.
Andreas did exceptionally ________ in his test, meaning that he qualifies for a scholarship.

**2** I hope to ________ this company as well as my father has for the last twenty years.
This popular soap opera is shown in 20 countries and has ________ for over 15 years.
The man arrested for the murder escaped from the police and is still on the ________.

**3** It struck me as ________ the way that Andrew never spoke about his past.
All the houses with ________ numbers are on the other side of the road.
In the twenty ________ years I've been living here we've always had good neighbours.

**4** Some critics of the Internet accuse it of being a ________ for corporate advertising.
The old lady claimed to be a ________ who could communicate with the dead.
The thief is described as being of ________ height and has several tattoos on his neck.

**5** He took a week off work with the express ________ of finding a new job.
I'm sure Tony deleted my file on ________, although he says it was an accident.
I don't mind living at home for now as it suits my ________ of saving money.

# Writing

CAE Part 1

## Formal letter

1 Read the following Writing Part 1 task.

You are finding it difficult to work in the library of the British university where you are studying. Read the extract from the library regulations, on which you have made some notes, and write a letter to the Library Director informing him/her of the reasons why it is difficult to study in the library and urging him/her to take action.

### UNIVERSITY LIBRARY REGULATIONS

*Conduct within the library*

- Silence must be maintained in all study areas of the library. — *why no specific regulations for mobile phones?*
- The playing of personal stereos or similar devices with headphones is not allowed. — *goes on all the time*
- Eating, drinking and smoking are forbidden, except in the specially designated areas. — *right next to study areas*

Any failure to observe these regulations should be reported to a member of staff. — *I have, but...*

*Student computing facilities*

- The library provides 55 PCs with Internet access for study purposes. — *not enough* The playing of games on the computers is prohibited. — *goes on all the time*

2 Write your **letter** in **180–220** words. You do not need to include postal addresses.

**Before you write**

Read the following pages in the Coursebook.
Formal letters: pages 194 to 195 in Ready for Writing.

# 9 Going places

## Reading

CAE Part 1

### Multiple choice

You are going to read three extracts which are all concerned in some way with travel. For questions **1–6**, choose the answer **(A**, **B**, **C** or **D)** which you think fits best according to the text.

### Extract from an online guidebook

You can legally drive in New Zealand for up to 12 months if you have either a current driver's licence from your home country or an International Driving Permit (IDP). After 12 months you are required to convert to a New Zealand licence. This applies to each visit to New Zealand. All drivers must carry their licence or permit at all times when driving. If your licence is not in English, you must bring an English translation with you or obtain an IDP. Contact your local automobile club for further details about obtaining one of these. It is important to note that if you are caught driving without either, you may be prosecuted for driving unlicensed or for driving without an appropriate licence and will be liable for an infringement fee of NZ$400, payable within 28 days, or up to NZ$1,000 on conviction in court.

Self-driving holidays are one of the most relaxing ways of enjoying New Zealand's landscape. Many of our roads are scenic and traffic is low when compared to international standards. Although New Zealand is a relatively small country it can take many hours to drive between cities and other destinations of interest. Even when distances are short, hilly or winding terrain or narrow secondary roads can slow your journey. If you're used to driving in the city, you should take care when driving on the open country roads. Weather extremes, one-lane bridges plus the kinds of road mentioned above require drivers to be very vigilant. Never drive if you are feeling tired, particularly after you have just completed a long-haul flight.

**1** According to the writer, foreign drivers in New Zealand
- **A** have to pay an instant fine if they do not have the correct licence.
- **B** will need to apply for a New Zealand licence after a year's stay.
- **C** must be able to show their licence even when not driving.
- **D** cannot use a licence issued by their own country for short visits.

**2** In the second paragraph, the overall purpose of the writer is to
- **A** recommend areas of New Zealand that are worth seeing.
- **B** suggest the best time for going on a self-driving holiday.
- **C** warn visitors against using unsafe countryside roads.
- **D** give advice regarding safe driving practices.

## Extract from a travel book

I found a deck chair at the edge of the sea. I could hear small lapping sounds beside me, as if a kindly monster was taking discreet sips of water from a large goblet. A few birds were waking up and beginning to career through the air in matinal excitement. Behind me, the raffia roofs of the hotel bungalows were visible through gaps in the trees. Before me was a view that I recognized from the brochure: the beach stretched away in a gentle curve towards the tip of the bay, behind it were jungle-covered hills, and the first row of coconut trees inclined irregularly towards the turquoise sea, as though some of them were craning their necks to catch a better angle of the sun.

Yet this description only imperfectly reflects what occurred within me that morning, for my attention was in truth far more fractured and confused than the foregoing paragraphs suggest. I may have noticed a few birds careering through the air (in matinal excitement) but my awareness of them was weakened by a number of other incongruous and unrelated elements, among these, a sore throat that I had developed during the flight, a worry at not having informed a colleague that I would be away, a pressure across both temples and a rising need to visit the bathroom. A momentous but until then overlooked fact was making its first appearance: that I had inadvertently brought myself with me to the island.

**3** In the first paragraph, what does the writer suggest about his holiday location?
- **A** It made him feel as if he were cut off from reality.
- **B** It matched the image he had previously had of it.
- **C** It appeared to offer him the quiet privacy he had hoped for.
- **D** It may not have been as safe and friendly as it seemed.

**4** Which of the following best summarizes the writer's point in the second paragraph?
- **A** There are aspects of daily life that cannot be ignored on holiday.
- **B** Only certain types of people can fully relax on holiday.
- **C** It is easier to notice the details in your surroundings on holiday.
- **D** It is better to share holiday experiences with companions.

## Extract from a photography book

Even though there is snow on the ground outside my home in Maryland, I'm sitting with Claude Monet on a sunny terrace behind a cottage set amidst a panoply of greenery along the Canal Nivernais in France. No matter that the impressionist master is dead or that I'm separated from summer in France by an ocean, two seasons, and a slew of logistical and financial issues. Thanks to Anne Keiser's photograph of that ivy-covered cottage, I'm seated in a white wrought-iron chair on a waterside terrace in the middle of a Monet painting.

Every time I look at that photo that ornate piece of garden furniture transfixes me. The chair is what the French writer Roland Barthes, in his book *Camera Lucida*, called the 'punctum' of a photograph, an element which 'rises from the scene, shoots out of it like an arrow and pierces me.' The punctum is something we add to the photograph that is nonetheless already there. The chair opens up an imaginary space which I fill with my desire to be sitting there, enjoying the sunlight and the scenery of a summer day in France, occupying a place in a living artwork.

**5** What point is exemplified by the references to the painter Claude Monet?
- **A** Good art is as meaningful now as in the past.
- **B** Some styles are often copied by other artists.
- **C** Artists are not as important as the art they create.
- **D** Certain images help people imagine they are elsewhere.

**6** In this piece, the writer is
- **A** comparing the talents of two types of artists.
- **B** showing the advantages of photography over painting.
- **C** implying that travel is more fulfilling than everyday matters.
- **D** explaining the effect of an aspect of photography.

# Vocabulary

Wordlist on page 213 of the Coursebook.

## Doing things alone

Match each sentence beginning **1–8** with an appropriate ending **a–h**.

**1** Media tycoon Wilson McShane is the archetypal **self-made**
**2** With nearly 5,000 head of cattle, the island is **self-sufficient**
**3** We read about the nautical achievements of **single-handed**
**4** The ex-vocalist with *The Recluses* has released her first **solo**
**5** At a table in the far corner of the empty pub sat the **solitary**
**6** KTL Airlines charge a forty-pound fee for **unaccompanied**
**7** The star is too far away to be clearly visible to the **unaided**
**8** The railway was built to serve the area's numerous **isolated**

**a** **children** travelling on all international and domestic flights.
**b** **figure** of Ed Glen, sipping at his regular Monday morning pint of bitter.
**c** **millionaire**, who started out as tea boy in the company he now owns.
**d** **album**, containing cover versions of great jazz songs from the fifties.
**e** **communities**, at a time when the horse was the only other form of transport.
**f** **yachtswoman** Ellen MacArthur in Unit 1 of the Coursebook.
**g** **in milk production**, and is able to export cheese to the mainland.
**h** **eye**, so a good telescope or pair of binoculars is recommended.

### Self help

Study the collocations in bold in the exercise above for one minute. Then cover the sentence endings a–h and look only at the beginnings 1–8. How many collocations can you remember?

## Criticism

1 The following adjectives and verbs are all collocates of the nouns ***criticism***. Underline the item in each group which does not express a similar meaning to the word(s) in bold. There is an example at the beginning **(0)**.

**0 increasing**
damaging (underlined)
growing
mounting

**1 a lot of**
considerable
constructive
widespread

**2 strong**
fierce
severe
valid

**3 not affected by**
impervious to
unmoved by
upset by

**4 give**
arouse
express
voice

**5 encounter**
come in for
meet with
respond to

**6 deal successfully with**
draw
overcome
withstand

2 Choose the correct option **A**, **B**, **C** or **D**.

**1** Her ______ criticism of his work, which was based purely on her intense dislike of him, served only to undermine his self-confidence.
**A** fierce **B** valid **C** constructive **D** widespread

**2** The President remained ______ by mounting criticism of his leadership and pressed ahead regardless with his controversial programme of policies.
**A** upset **B** unmoved **C** impervious **D** overcome

**3** Police chiefs yesterday ______ strong criticism of a judge's decision to give a man convicted of armed robbery a six-month suspended sentence.
**A** attracted **B** met with **C** aroused **D** voiced

**4** The decision to site the nuclear power station next to the nature reserve ______ widespread criticism from opposition politicians and environmental groups.
**A** came in **B** responded to **C** drew **D** expressed

## Word formation

1 Write the correct form of the word in capitals on the right so that it collocates with each word or words in the group on the left. There is an example at the beginning **(0)**.

| | | | |
|---|---|---|---|
| **0** *timeless* | quality<br>appeal<br>classic | | **TIME** |
| **1** | maintain<br>lose your<br>regain | ___________ | **COMPOSE** |
| **2** | cause considerable<br>suffer great<br>overcome economic | ___________ | **HARD** |
| **3** ___________ | role<br>evidence<br>actress | | **SUPPORT** |
| **4** | show proof of<br>reveal someone's<br>a case of mistaken | ___________ | **IDENTIFY** |
| **5** | competition<br>winning<br>dictionary | ___________ | **ENTER** |

2 Complete each of the gaps with one of the collocations from exercise 1. You may need to change some of the words. There is an example at the beginning **(0)**.

**0** Many of Disney's early films are *timeless classics*, which continue to be enjoyed even now in the modern computer age.

**1** A photograph of the ________________ in this year's *Inventor of the Future* competition will be printed in the April edition of *Science Today* magazine.

**2** Catherine Zeta-Jones won an Oscar for Best ________________ for her role in the film *Chicago*.

**3** Joseph Rendell was arrested in what seems to have been ________________ ; police are still looking for a Joseph Randall in connection with the robbery.

**4** He was visibly shocked at the news; it was a while before he ________________ and was calm enough to ask how it had happened.

**5** The dramatic increase in house prices and rents has ________________ to those on low incomes.

# Language focus

Grammar reference on page 223 of the Coursebook.

## Creating emphasis

In each of the following sentences there is a word which should not be there. Cross out the word. There is an example at the beginning **(0)**.

**0** What annoys me so much about her is the fact ~~of~~ that she never helps with the washing up.

**1** It was just after we arrived at the hotel that we have received a call from our neighbour telling us we'd been burgled.

**2** I used to hate going to visit my grandparents: all what we ever did was watch television and listen to my grandad talking about politics.

**3** It might have been because Jane that rang when I was in the shower – she's the only person I know who'd phone so early in the day.

**4** It's not so much what she says that annoys me, and it's more the way she says it.

**5** He realized he had little hope of finding his way out of the forest in the fog, so what he did it was to build himself a shelter out of branches and leaves.

**6** It was only when the police came at 3 o'clock in the morning so that they finally turned their music down.

## Use of English

CAE Part 1

### Multiple-choice cloze

For questions **1–12**, read the text below and then decide which answer **(A**, **B**, **C** or **D)** best fits each gap. There is an example at the beginning **(0)**.

### Lost luggage

You get off your plane and **(0)** ______ your way to the Baggage Reclaim area, where you locate the carousel for your flight and wait patiently for your luggage. After quite some time spent waiting, there is no **(1)** ______ of your bags and you begin to consider the possibility that they may have gone **(2)** ______. What should you do?

Firstly, don't panic. The most likely **(3)** ______ is that your bags simply didn't make it onto the flight, perhaps because they were mislaid at the departure airport, or perhaps because the aircraft had already **(4)** ______ its weight allowance. If they **(5)** ______ to appear on the carousel, report the loss before you leave the baggage hall and go through customs. **(6)** ______ your luggage should be no problem, provided you've kept **(7)** ______ of your baggage checks - those little barcodes stuck to the back of your tickets at check-in.

Go to the handling agent's desk and **(8)** ______ a Property Irregularity Report (PIR) form, which describes the checked bag and its **(9)** ______. Then, ask the baggage-services manager for a contact telephone number and confirm that your bags will be forwarded to your final **(10)** ______.

Most bags **(11)** ______ up within a day or two, but if yours never show (and it may be weeks before the airline accepts that they are permanently lost), you can claim **(12)** ______ from the airline.

| | | | |
|---|---|---|---|
| **0 A** go | **B** get | **C** <u>make</u> | **D** walk |
| **1 A** indication | **B** sign | **C** notice | **D** mark |
| **2 A** lost | **B** missing | **C** absent | **D** misplaced |
| **3 A** example | **B** understanding | **C** clarification | **D** explanation |
| **4 A** surpassed | **B** overtaken | **C** exceeded | **D** outdone |
| **5 A** lack | **B** omit | **C** avoid | **D** fail |
| **6 A** Retracing | **B** Retaining | **C** Recovering | **D** Reinstating |
| **7 A** control | **B** hold | **C** property | **D** hand |
| **8 A** carry out | **B** complete | **C** fulfil | **D** realize |
| **9 A** contents | **B** inside | **C** filling | **D** packing |
| **10 A** destiny | **B** destination | **C** termination | **D** terminus |
| **11 A** come | **B** turn | **C** bring | **D** put |
| **12 A** refund | **B** reparation | **C** amendment | **D** compensation |

CAE Part 2

## Open cloze

For questions **1–15**, read the text below and think of the word which best fits each gap. Use only **one** word in each gap. There is an example at the beginning **(0)**.

### The revolution in the way we travel

Less than a decade **(0)** _ago_ , mainstream travel agencies reigned supreme over a booming holiday industry. Only they had the technology which **(1)** _____ search the reservations systems of airlines, hotels and package-holiday firms. Many were **(2)** ____ more than order-takers but enjoyed a 10 per cent commission **(3)** _________ package tours. But **(4)** ______ days have gone. Travel and the Internet are made **(5)** ________ one another, connecting a global inventory of seats, beds and rental cars with millions of travellers, all with individual needs and all now with the power to book for themselves. Even the traditional package tour operators, **(6)** ________ their own chains of retailers, are now offering online discounts **(7)** ________ undercut their travel agencies. **(8)** ________ if agents were willing to take a cut in commission, it would do them little good. Hundreds of agencies are still going to close **(9)** ________ a result of the recent consolidation of the big four UK holiday firms into the big two. The future for mainstream travel agents looks bleak, **(10)** ________ they can add value by offering real expertise. It is this sort of knowledge that companies **(11)** ________ as Travel Counsellors use to market themselves. **(12)** ________ recruiting experienced agents and equipping them with the technology necessary for telephone sales, they **(13)** ________ offer customers a professional service **(14)** ________ the comfort of their own home. Catering for a new market of people that have not been near a travel agency **(15)** _____ they first acquired a broadband connection may be the only way to survive for tour operators.

CAE Part 3

## Word formation

For questions **1–10**, read the text below. Use the word given in capitals at the end of some of the lines to form a word that fits in the gap **in the same line**. There is an example at the beginning **(0)**.

### Women only

| | |
|---|---|
| **(0)** _Increasingly_ , women are taking their holidays without men. For | **INCREASE** |
| **(1)** ___________ reasons, camaraderie or just plain fun, a growing number of female | **SAFE** |
| tourists are signing up for women-only trips. Twenty years ago only a **(2)** ___________ | **HAND** |
| of companies offered such holidays; now there are several hundred. Travel | |
| **(3)** ___________ Andrea Littlewood says that the combination of higher incomes with | **CONSULT** |
| delayed marriage, divorce, retirement and widowhood has **(4)** ___________ more | **ABLE** |
| women to travel, often on their own. They are attracted by the sense of **(5)** ___________ | **FREE** |
| that a holiday without men affords them. 'Women in a group tend to feel **(6)** ___________ | **INHIBIT** |
| and speak more openly than when men are around,' she adds. 'Even on energy-sapping | |
| adventure holidays the atmosphere is relaxed and **(7)** ___________ . It's also a great deal | **COOPERATE** |
| more fun. Women laugh more **(8)** ___________ than men, probably because they don't | **READY** |
| mind laughing at themselves.' Since her divorce Janice Cummings has been a regular | |
| traveller with Everywoman Tours, an Oxford-based Company whose very name is a | |
| **(9)** ___________ to men. 'And a good thing too,' she says. 'Men simply cannot resist the | **DETER** |
| **(10)** ___________ to try and take control, no matter where they are. And that | **TEMPT** |
| includes on holiday. Thankfully, there is none of that with Everywoman.' | |

CAE Part 5

## Key word transformations

For questions **1–8**, complete the second sentence so that it has a similar meaning to the first sentence, using the word given. **Do not change the word given.** You must use between **three** and **six** words, including the word given. Here is an example **(0)**.

**0** I first noticed the good-looking French backpacker while I was looking at some brochures.

**LOOK**

It was *while I was having a look* at some brochures that I first noticed the good-looking French backpacker.

1 I didn't stop worrying about the wild animals until we were safe inside camp.

**ONLY**

It was ______________________ safety of camp that I stopped worrying about the wild animals.

**2** Steve's one topic of conversation is the time he spent as a pilot.

**EVER**

The time he spent as a pilot ______________________ about.

**3** After arriving at the airport, we realized that our passports were still at home.

**UNTIL**

It ______________________ at the airport that we realized our passports were still at home.

**4** When Michael's boat began to sink, he sent a signal for help.

**DID**

When Michael's boat began to sink, what ______________________ a signal for help.

**5** Immediately after Emi quit her job, she booked a package tour around Europe.

**HAD**

As ______________________ in her notice Emi booked a package tour around Europe.

**6** I don't get on very well with many people but I hit it off with Jason straightaway.

**TOOK**

I don't get on very well with many people but Jason ______________________ other straightaway.

**7** I was impatient to get home because the holiday was such a disaster.

**WAIT**

The holiday was so ______________________ to get home.

**8** I was hoping not to have to share a tent with anyone else on the camping trip.

**TO**

I was hoping I would ______________________ myself on the camping trip but I had to share.

# Writing

CAE Part 1

## Report

1 Read the following Writing Part 1 task.

You are the secretary of the Student Committee at a language school in Brighton, England. The Events Organizer has written to you about last term's social programme. Read the extract from the Events Organizer's email and the comments from students on the social programme and write a report for the Events Organizer.

To: Secretary of Student Committee
From: Elisa Burrows, Events Organizer
Re: Autumn Term Programme

Could you write a report for me on last term's activities? I'd like to know what students thought of the social and cultural events and the weekend excursions. Please indicate what they did and didn't like, and include some suggestions for improvements.

Many thanks

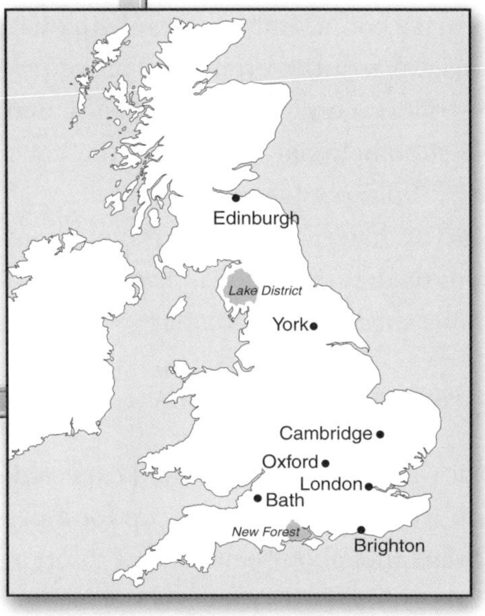


*Everyone enjoyed the social events (eg karaoke, beach barbecues). How about including team sports?*

*The topics of the cultural talks were boring – no wonder they were poorly attended.*

*The cultural trips to London museums, theatres etc were too pricey for me. A pity, because they looked really interesting.*

*Loved the weekend coach excursions to Edinburgh, York and the Lake District. A bit far, though.*

2 Decide whether the following statements are true (T) or false (F).

**Content**

**1** It is not advisable to build on the information given in the input material by adding points of your own.

**Organization and cohesion**

**2** Either of the following two plans would be acceptable.

| **Plan A** | **Plan B** |
|---|---|
| Introduction | Introduction |
| Social events: positive & negative aspect(s) | Positive aspects |
| Cultural events: positive & negative aspect(s) | Negative aspects |
| Weekend excursions: positive & negative aspect(s) | Suggestions for improvements |
| Suggestions for improvements | |

**3** An overall heading and individual paragraph headings are completely unnecessary.

**Range of language**

**4** The language of recommendation would be useful here.

**Target reader and register**

**5** The register will depend on your interpretation of your relationship with the Events Organizer, but it must be consistent.

3 Write your **report** in **180–220** words.

# 10 House and home

## Reading

CAE Part 4

### Multiple matching

1 You are going to read a set of magazine interviews with four teachers about their flat-sharing experiences. For questions **1–15**, choose from the interviews (**A–D**). The interviews may be chosen more than once.

**Of which teacher are the following statements true?**

I might look for a flatmate in the right circumstances. **1** ____
Finding a flatmate now would represent a backward step to me. **2** ____
I suspect my flatmate considered my behaviour to be odd. **3** ____
It is necessary to make compromises when living with other people. **4** ____
Talking about housework duties eventually proved to be pointless. **5** ____
There were no restrictions on when I could leave and return home. **6** ____
I did not feel obliged to help out much with the housework. **7** ____
I would feel guilty if I did not pay my way. **8** ____
It became necessary to have a frank discussion about housework. **9** ____
It was important to us that the flat was easily affordable. **10** ____
Sharing a flat can be successful as long as the flatmates have something in common. **11** ____
I was less comfortable after others in the house began to depend on me financially. **12** ____
Setting up in a flat was not as easy as I had expected. **13** ____
My flatmate's hard work in the flat made up for a personality flaw. **14** ____
I felt obliged to keep quiet about behaviour I disapproved of. **15** ____

## Two's company, three's a crowd?

**Flat-sharing has long been a tradition in New Zealand, and not just for students. But while there are those who love the sense of communal living, there are others who can't wait to establish their own private nest. Lisa Simpson speaks to four teachers.**

### A Craig Andrews

The flat-sharing experience has not always been a rewarding one for New Zealander Craig Andrews. There was, for instance, the time when Craig found himself flat-sharing in Rome while teaching for a language school. 'The other tenant, an English man, was also working for them. The big issue was that he was totally uninterested in cleaning. Despite the great many hints I dropped, he never picked up on them, and so it was all left to me. In retrospect, I suppose he might have thought I was rather obsessive with my constant cleaning.' Craig felt it necessary to put up with the situation as their contract with the school had six months to run and he felt that any confrontation would have ultimately led to greater tension. Craig learnt a valuable lesson from this experience, which ensured that living arrangements with future flatmates were more harmonious. 'Provided flatmates' backgrounds are similar and their interests compatible, there's no reason why it all shouldn't work out well,' he says. 'And just establish the rules from the outset.' Now a house-owner, however, Craig admits that he can't imagine ever being in a flat-sharing situation again. 'I realize it's cheaper but I prefer my privacy and I'm not prepared to give that up.'

## B Derene Els

Having emigrated to New Zealand from South Africa four years ago, Derene is currently living with her family. 'I pay rent which I know some people might find strange, but it would be morally wrong not to, especially as I'm working.' She feels that she has her own privacy to a certain extent but says that 'taking turns with the television remote control, meeting halfway when it comes to the bathroom schedule, settling for the smaller room when you really want the big one – this is what you have to do when you're all under the same roof.' Derene is currently keeping an eye out for a small apartment. Her criteria is simply 'near the coast' as she needs a sense of open space around her. Perhaps this is what drew her to Australia where she took time off from her job in New Zealand to work as a translator. After that contract came to an end, she decided to stay on with the host family who'd been putting her up. 'Once the arrangement became more formal, when I felt they were relying on me for income, I was not so at ease,' she explains. 'But I still felt obliged to be sociable and didn't want to appear rude by keeping myself to myself. All the same, I could still come and go as I wished and the door was never locked.'

## C Sarah Nuttall

Originally from the UK, Sarah has spent the last five years in New Zealand. She's found the local flat-sharing experience rather different to what she was used to. 'There aren't so many flats available here,' she explains. 'As well as this, in London the flats are usually fully furnished whereas in New Zealand you only get a cooker. When my boyfriend and I first got here, it had never occurred to us that we would have to go out and buy loads of second-hand stuff just to get started.' She's adamant that there's no room for a third person in her flat. 'We've talked about getting an extra person in to reduce costs but our privacy comes first. But if I were ever single again, I suppose I'd consider it. It would be a good way of meeting friends.' Sarah's first flat-sharing experience was in London with four friends she'd been to university with. She admits that there were both good and bad times. 'We hardly ever argued at first except for minor quarrels over the washing up.' Eventually, however, things came to a head when the kitchen became unusable. 'We had a group meeting and the rules were laid down. They were effective for about three weeks and then things went back to the way they were.'

## D Callum McNab

Now in the complicated process of looking for his own house, Callum spent his second year of university flat-sharing with three other students. There was a unanimous decision that the accommodation had to be within their financial means and in close proximity to the university. 'There were no real disputes. One woman, Cathy, was extremely talkative, so much so you'd end up not listening. But she was generous and she very much pulled her weight around the flat so we could live with that.' Callum confesses to little participation when it came to housework. 'There were times when we'd all pitch in but the problem was that I spent a lot of time away from the flat. It was agreed that I wasn't as responsible for the messes created and I wasn't going to argue with that.' When that flat got sold, Callum found the easiest option was to move in with his brother. 'I can't say I had that much in common with him, except for our interest in foreign movies.' And now the flat-sharing seems to be coming to an end? 'I couldn't imagine flat-sharing ever again. Living with a stranger would mean I'd failed in some way, like I was de-maturing.'

2 Complete the gaps with the correct form of one of the expressions in the box. All the expressions appeared in the reading text.

| | | | | |
|---|---|---|---|---|
| come to | come to an end | come to a head | come first | come and go |

1 Of course my work is important, but my family always ________________ .

2 I can do the ironing or clean the house, but when it ________________ cooking, I'm absolutely useless.

3 Tensions had been steadily increasing, and things ________________ last week when riots broke out and the government was forced to act.

4 Her parents have given her a key, so she can ________________ as she pleases.

5 You can see that summer is ________________ ; the leaves have started falling off the trees already.

# Vocabulary

Wordlist on page 214 of the Coursebook.

1 In **A** and **B** complete each gap with one of the words from the boxes.

**A**

| bee | dog | owl | lion | mouse |
|---|---|---|---|---|

**1** I was woken up at two o'clock by an inconsiderate _______ **hooting** monotonously in the tree next to my tent.

**2** We heard the **squeaking** of a _______ coming from the cupboard where we had set the trap.

**3** A honey _______ came **buzzing** past, a sign that spring had at last arrived.

**4** The neighbours' _______ spends the day **whining** and scratching at the door while they're both out at work.

**5** What's the name of the company that has that _______ **roaring** before the beginning of each film?

**B**

| leaves | floorboards | stomach | drum | music |
|---|---|---|---|---|

**1** His ____________ **rumbled**, reminding him that he hadn't eaten since lunchtime.

**2** The ____________ **rustled** in the gentle breeze.

**3** I wish that child would stop **banging** that ____________ !

**4** *You* can't complain – you have your ____________ **blaring out** all day.

**5** We heard voices and the sound of footsteps on **creaking** ____________ .

2 Choose the correct answer **A**, **B**, **C** or **D**.

**1** He's a very well-behaved little boy – I rarely have to __________ my voice to him.
**A** shout **B** lose **C** raise **D** lift

**2** As we climbed higher, the noise of the traffic gradually __________ away.
**A** faded **B** left **C** grew **D** weakened

**3** I couldn't hear what they were saying; they were in the next room so their voices were __________ .
**A** booming **B** muffled **C** hoarse **D** rough

**4** She came in, picked up her things, and left before I could __________ a sound.
**A** pronounce **B** tell **C** express **D** utter

**5** There was a __________ party going on next door last night; the police eventually came at half past one and put a stop to it.
**A** constant **B** continuous **C** roomy **D** rowdy

**6** He proposed to her in the _______ lit restaurant of the hotel with piano music playing in the background.
**A** soundly **B** softly **C** smoothly **D** sparsely

**7** Cleaners worked overtime to get the place looking spick and _______ for the presidential visit.
**A** spam **B** spot **C** spin **D** span

**8** Factory workers lived in council flats which were _______ built and badly maintained.
**A** poorly **B** weakly **C** highly **D** slightly

**9** Immigrants live in _______ conditions, with up to 15 sharing a small room.
**A** spacious **B** cramped **C** restrained **D** constrained

**10** The town is ideally _______ for visiting both London and the south coast.
**A** set **B** centred **C** orientated **D** situated

## Language focus

Grammar reference on page 223 of the Coursebook.

### Participle clauses

Combine the following pairs of sentences using participle clauses.

***Examples:***

Sheffield FC was founded in 1857. This makes it the oldest football club in the world.
*Sheffield FC was founded in 1857, making it the oldest football club in the world.*

He inherited a huge sum of money from his grandmother. He decided to give up work.
*Having inherited a huge sum of money from his grandmother, he decided to give up work.*

**1** 'Lord of the Rings: Return of the King' won 11 Oscars. It equalled the record held by 'Ben Hur' and 'Titanic' for the highest number of Academy Awards.

**2** We finally discovered where the leak was. We called in a plumber.

**3** The school now has 1,254 students. This represents a 6% increase on last year's figure.

**4** Part of the stadium roof collapsed. It injured six spectators.

**5** I am not a parent. I can take my holidays whenever I like.

**6** The team has had a disastrous season so far. It has won only three of its last sixteen games.

**7** Our parents went away for the weekend. My brother and I had a party.

**8** I was walking home from school yesterday. I bumped into Alex.

## Use of English

CAE Part 3

### Word formation

For questions **1–10**, use the word given in capitals at the end of some of the lines to form a word that fits in the gap **in the same line**. There is an example at the beginning **(0)**.

| Treehouses | |
|---|---|
| In some of Britain's most exclusive **(0)** *neighbourhoods* where swimming | **NEIGHBOUR** |
| pools and conservatories are commonplace, the most stylish are opting for | |
| the only addition **(1)** _______ to turn the neighbours green - a luxury treehouse | **GUARANTEE** |
| for adults. **(2)** _______ more than £20,000, they come with drinks cabinets, | **COST** |
| dining tables, **(3)** _______ kitchens and balconies. Some owners find their | **FIT** |
| treehouses are perfect for holding **(4)** _______ business meetings, and one | **INTERRUPT** |
| businessman liked his so much that he made it into a permanent office. | |
| Derek and Edwina Lilley spent £24,000 on Britain's most **(5)** _________ and | **LUXURY** |
| extravagant treehouse. It took four weeks to build and can accommodate | |
| 35 for drinks parties with ease. It has a kitchen **(6)** _______ with a combination | **EQUIP** |
| oven, grill and hob, as well as hot and cold **(7)** _______ water. Malcolm and | **RUN** |
| Sarah Le May had a two-storey treehouse built at their home in Hampshire, | |
| surrounded by a balcony, with **(8)** _______ views of the countryside. 'It is the | **BREATH** |
| ideal place to sit with a glass of wine at the end of the day as you look out at | |
| the **(9)** _______,' said Sarah. The upper-crust treehouses are the product of | **SUN** |
| Scottish company called Peartree, which built 50 in its first year. Planning | |
| **(10)** _______ is not needed as they are regarded as temporary buildings. | **PERMIT** |

CAE Part 1

## Multiple-choice cloze

For questions **1–12**, read the text below and then decide which answer **(A**, **B**, **C** or **D)** best fits each gap. There is an example at the beginning **(0)**.

### Flat to Let

**Location:** Norfolk Gardens, Westgate

**No. of bedrooms:** 1

**Price per week:** £420

This large one-bedroomed flat, situated in the **(0)** _______ residential suburb of Westgate and **(1)** _______ the nearby St John's Park, is ideal for a busy single person or couple. The accommodation is **(2)** _______ located in the heart of the suburb within **(3)** _______ walking distance of the wide range of amenities offered by both Westgate and the fashionable Donatello Road Market.

**(4)** _______ decorated and carpeted, the property **(5)** _______ a double bedroom, good-sized reception room, large living room, **(6)** _______ fitted kitchen and a bathroom with quality shower. Tenants also have **(7)** _______ of their own secure underground parking space. The flat is simply but **(8)** _______ furnished and the south-facing living room is pleasantly light and **(9)** _______ , with large picture windows which offer superb views of the surrounding area.

What **(10)** _______ this property apart from other accommodation with similar **(11)** _______ is its very acceptable price, given its central location and excellent transport links to other parts of the city. For **(12)** _______ details or to arrange a viewing telephone 020 786 50990.

| | | | | |
|---|---|---|---|---|
| **0** | **A** greenish | **B** <u>leafy</u> | **C** flowering | **D** blooming |
| **1** | **A** overseeing | **B** overhanging | **C** overlooking | **D** overreaching |
| **2** | **A** appropriately | **B** fittingly | **C** suitably | **D** conveniently |
| **3** | **A** easy | **B** simple | **C** close | **D** nearby |
| **4** | **A** Newly | **B** Lately | **C** Ultimately | **D** Proximately |
| **5** | **A** composes | **B** comprises | **C** comprehends | **D** compounds |
| **6** | **A** absolutely | **B** extremely | **C** fully | **D** entirely |
| **7** | **A** service | **B** employment | **C** application | **D** use |
| **8** | **A** sparsely | **B** plainly | **C** richly | **D** tastefully |
| **9** | **A** draughty | **B** breezy | **C** airy | **D** gusty |
| **10** | **A** sets | **B** puts | **C** keeps | **D** holds |
| **11** | **A** types | **B** kinds | **C** characteristics | **D** aspects |
| **12** | **A** added | **B** advanced | **C** further | **D** larger |

CAE Part 4

## Gapped sentences

For questions **1–5** below, think of **one** word only which can be used appropriately in all three sentences. In this exercise, the words required can be found in the article *Housework Gets You Down* on page 129 of the Coursebook. Here is an example **(0)**.

**0** I don't see the _point_ of having a second meeting to discuss the same thing.
It's important to _point_ out that not all the events in the book are based on fact.
I believe the final _point_ on the agenda this morning is the matter of a pay increase.

**1** The guidebook is __________ with many useful maps and lists of cheap places to stay.
Each team had to __________ their task within 30 minutes to stay in the competition.
It took me ages to __________ the forms I needed for my visa.

**2** New Zealand was the first country in the world to give women the __________ to vote.
That car has parked __________ behind you so be careful when you reverse.
I don't think that finishing a relationship by text message is the __________ way to do it.

**3** I last saw Marta getting on a ship that was __________ for Spain.
Knowing John, he's __________ to be late for the meeting.
The bank robbers had __________ the hostages together with rope.

**4** Could you __________ me how to use this photocopier if you have time today?
All this rain we're having just goes to __________ that climate change is really happening.
If we wait a bit longer, I'm sure Yuri will __________ up eventually with another excuse for being late.

**5** If you want to __________ the flight, you won't have time to check your luggage in.
I'm afraid we don't have any replacement parts for this __________ of camera.
Listening to love songs after a break-up tends to __________ me depressed.

CAE Part 5

## Key word transformations

Complete the second sentence so that it has a similar meaning to the first sentence, using the word given. **Do not change the word given**. You must use between **three** and **six** words, including the word given. Here is an example **(0)**.

**0** The police asked Mr Porter many questions about exactly where he was on the night of his wife's murder.
**RELATION**
The police asked Mr Porter many questions _in relation to his exact_ whereabouts on the night of his wife's murder.

**1** As I didn't want to disappoint my parents, I agreed to go to medical school.
**LET**
Not ____________________ my parents, I agreed to go to medical school.

**2** After deciding he would leave home, Enrique immediately began searching for an apartment.
**DECISION**
Having ____________________ leave home, Enrique immediately began searching for an apartment.

**3** Make sure you look after your bag in this café as there are many thieves around.
**EYE**
I suggest ____________________ your bag in this café as there are many thieves around.

**4** Your chances of being affected by eye-strain and back injury increase with the amount of time you spend in front of a screen.
**LIKELY**
The more time you spend in front of a screen, the ____________________from eye-strain and back injury.

5 With that bad cold you won't be able to help us so take the day off work.
**USE**
With that bad cold you'll ______________ anyone so take the day off work.

6 When James heard that his father had left all his money to his brother he did not find it surprising.
**AS**
It __________________ to hear that his father had left all his money to his brother.

7 I feel certain that there will be a new government after the election.
**BOUND**
In my opinion, there____________________ of government after the election.

8 Most employees used to be proud of working for the same company all their lives but not anymore.
**PRIDE**
Most employees no _________________ working for the same company all their lives.

# Writing

CAE Part 2

## Contribution to a brochure

1 Read the following Writing Part 2 task and the model below.

A brochure is being produced in English aimed at encouraging foreign visitors to spend their holidays in your country. You have been asked to write an entry on the type of accommodation available for those people wishing to enjoy a countryside holiday. You should include information on at least two different types of accommodation, pointing out the positive features of each type and giving a general idea of prices.

Write your **entry** for the brochure in **220–260** words.

**Countryside Accommodation**

If your aim in coming to our country is to get away from it all, the choice of rural accommodation is wide, with something to suit every pocket.

**Campsites**

In the lower price bracket are the many campsites to be found in some of our most beautiful rural areas. These are generally situated well away from busy towns, guaranteeing peace and quiet and a well earned rest from the hustle and bustle of everyday life. Most cater for children, offering a range of facilities designed to provide weary parents with a welcome break.

Prices vary depending on the campsite and the type of accommodation you choose. A family of four with their own tent in a three-star campsite can pay as little as 300 Euros for a week in the high season. A rather more expensive option is to hire a caravan, which works out at about 90 Euros a night but accommodates up to 6 people.

**Rural Houses**

If comfort is a major factor when choosing accommodation and money is no object, you could stay at one of the large number of rural houses located throughout the country. These are usually restored country houses or mansions, with all the benefits of a five-star hotel, but always in a peaceful countryside setting. And for those who like to be active on holiday, there are plenty of organized outdoor activities on offer, such as horse riding, hiking, canoeing or even paragliding.

Rural houses are clearly at the upper end of the price range, with a double room costing anywhere between 150 and 300 Euros per night, but if you really want to pamper yourself, there's no better way.

2 Underline those sections of the model which are used to talk about the positive features of the accommodation.

***Example:*** *to be found in some of our most beautiful rural areas*

3 In the box below write those expressions from the model which refer to price.

***Example:*** *with something to suit every pocket*

4 Circle any present and past participles which introduce participle clauses.

***Example:*** *guaranteeing peace and quiet*

5 Write an answer to the following Part 2 task:

A brochure is being produced in English aimed at encouraging foreign visitors to spend their holidays in your country. You have been asked to write an entry on the type of accommodation available for those people wishing to enjoy a holiday in the city or large town in which you live or which is nearest to your home. You should include information on at least two different types of accommodation, pointing out the positive features of each type and giving a general idea of prices.

Write your **entry** for the brochure in **220–260** words.

## Don't forget!

- Plan your answer before you write.
- Organize your ideas into logical paragraphs. Include a *brief* introduction.
- Use some of the language from the model when referring to price.
- Participle clauses add variety to your writing and help create a good impression.

## Before you write

- See page 199 in the Coursebook for more information and useful language for brochures and guidebooks.

The accommodation in the castle is well ventilated and allows you to experience nature at first hand.

# 11 A cultural education

## Reading

CAE Part 4

### Multiple matching

1 You are going to read a magazine article in which five men are interviewed about Paris. For questions **1–15**, choose from the people **(A–E)**. The men may be chosen more than once.

**Of which man are the following true?**

| | |
|---|---|
| He explains an established routine with guests. | **1** ____ |
| He admits that he only recently appreciated a certain aspect of Paris. | **2** ____ |
| He expresses regret that Paris is producing art work which is of average standard. | **3** ____ |
| He mentions a misunderstanding that was eventually resolved. | **4** ____ |
| He states that he has always maintained the same opinion of Paris. | **5** ____ |
| He comments on the importance of maintaining social customs. | **6** ____ |
| He believes that Parisians have strong opinions which they like to express. | **7** ____ |
| He feels that it is difficult for people to walk around Paris. | **8** ____ |
| He expresses regret that he will never belong to a particular group. | **9** ____ |
| He states that he feels more comfortable living in Paris than in his current city. | **10** ____ |
| He feels Paris could be more lively if more people from different ethnic backgrounds lived there. | **11** ____ |
| He comments that it is almost impossible to gain the approval of Parisians for your work. | **12** ____ |
| He mentions a sudden decision which proved to be the right one. | **13** ____ |
| He suggests that French art would benefit from foreign influences. | **14** ____ |
| He appreciates the way in which Paris can improve his mood. | **15** ____ |

# My Paris

***It's still the perfect cultural destination. So we asked those on intimate terms with the French capital to tell us what it means to them and to reveal their favourite places.***

**A *Gilbert Adair:*** writer

I lived in Paris in the late 1960s and through the 1970s. Although I've been back in London for the past 20 years or so, I still feel more at home there than I do here. I went native, I suppose. I tend to stay in Montparnasse, and what's curious about it is that even though it's 90 years since artists like Picasso and Modigliani were around, something of their spirit survives. Paris must be the only place where you see people on their own in a café, scribbling in a notepad. However, in a sense, in artistic terms, Paris is going through a rather mediocre period. Maybe it has something to do with attempts by the establishment to keep French art 'pure'; that is to say, not affected by any culture not French. Because of this, Paris has become something of a museum.

**B *Andreas Whittam Smith:*** editor

I first went there when I was 20. I thought that it was the most romantic city in the world and my view hasn't changed. I find it beautiful, the architecture particularly, and the way the long streets are always finished off with a building at the end of them. I don't enjoy the fact that it's a city that favours the motorist over the pedestrian, for whom it can be a challenge just to get about, to cross the road even. One of my favourite places in Paris is an emporium called *Deyrolle* on the *Rue du Bac*. They sell all kinds of geological specimens and butterflies. Every time we have people staying with us we take them there and they always buy something.

**C *Charles Darwent:*** art critic

The launderette by my flat in Belleville sums up Paris for me. You put your clothes in the machine and then, committing the machine's number to memory, you walk to a different machine in a different room and feed it coins. Someone could steal your stuff while this was going on but the beggar lady who lives there would stop them. Though she's barred from the café next door, she put in a good word for me with the owner. She told him the reason I had never greeted him in French on walking in wasn't because I was rude, but English. So he took to crossing the bar whenever I entered, shaking my hand and roaring '*Bonjour, Anglais*' until I gave in and began to pre-empt him. Now we get on famously. Paris is all about following ritual. Everything – from how you feed a washing machine, to the way you greet someone, or the way you enter a bar. There's a cafe near here where the customers spend hours discussing the food. They are pompous and ridiculous and I long to be one of them, and never will.

**D *Philippe Starck:*** interior designer

Despite being born in Paris, it was only a few years ago that I took a proper look at the city and truly saw its beauty. But it's not about the stone or the architecture; it's the people, the Parisians. The people are highly critical. No matter whether you make something good or bad, it will always be bad – they are very negative, which makes it the hardest place to create something. At the same time, it's their wonderful vigilance that creates some of the best quality in the world. For this I am grateful, although it took me six years to discover this secret. Parisians are also incredibly snobbish people – they create tribes and stick to them. There's one for music, one for art, one for journalists, and they like to fight each other. We could never just follow a leader – people are too independent-minded and aren't afraid to be frank.

**E *Douglas Kennedy:*** writer

In 1998, I was on a book tour, and staying in a hotel. I spent the whole night walking and ended up in the *Place de la Concorde* at 6am, just in time for sunrise. The whole place was completely deserted. and not a car to be seen. I thought to myself, I have to live here and so I bought a flat in St Germain. It was spontaneous, I suppose, but it turned out very well. You can live a proper urban life in Paris: within five minutes' walk from your door there can be at least 15 cinemas and several excellent markets. No matter how depressed I feel, or how bad the writing is going, the sight of the city makes me feel better. It is much more compact than London, so even though you can never find a cab at night, you can always find your way home. There is, however, not the multi-cultural buzz you get in London: I think this robs the city of a certain dynamism.

2 Complete each collocation in **A** with a noun, and each phrasal verb in **B** with a particle. The words you need all appeared in the reading text on page 85. There is an example at the beginning of each exercise **(0)**.

**A Collocations**

**0** I wish I'd had time to **take a proper** _look_ **at** the contract – I'd never have signed it if I had. (D)

**1** The company is **going through a rather difficult** ________ at the moment and many predict that redundancies will be made. (A)

**2** My host family were very welcoming and made me **feel** very much **at** ________. (A)

**3** For homework we often had to **commit** a poem **to** ________ and then recite it in class a week later. (C)

**4** My neighbour works at Tibbenhams; she **put in a good** ________ **for** me **with** the boss, and he gave me a job. (C)

**5** Bess, a three-year-old sheep dog that got lost while on holiday with his owners, has managed to **find her** ________ **home** – nearly 200 miles away! (E)

**B Phrasal verbs**

**0** There's too much traffic on the roads – the best way to **get** _about_ the city is by underground. (B)

**1** My teenage niece has some very unusual habits – she's recently **taken** ________ calling everyone 'mate' – including me! (C)

**2** That type of uninformed remark **sums** ________ the Prime Minister – he is completely out of touch with reality. (C)

**3** They couldn't bear the sight of each other at first, but now they **get** ________ famously. (C)

**4** There were a few problems during rehearsals but it all **turned** ________ well in the end, and the play was a great success. (E)

**5** We wanted to go to Birmingham, but we got on the wrong train and **ended** ________ in Crewe. (E)

3 Check your answers to exercise 2 in the reading text on page 85. The letters in brackets refer to the paragraphs in which each answer can be found.

## Vocabulary

Wordlist on page 214 of the Coursebook.

### Sight

Underline the correct alternative.

**1** Icy roads and **poor** *visibility/sight/view* due to fog meant driving conditions were extremely dangerous.

**2** I've always **had poor** *eyesight/view/look*, whereas my brother, who's fifty-six, still **has twenty-twenty** *vision/eye/sight* and will probably never have to wear glasses.

**3** I'd hate to be a film star, always **in the public** *vision/eye/show*, recognized wherever you go.

**4** As soon as I mentioned Sally, Paul **gave me a knowing** *sight/view/look*. 'But Sally and I are just good friends,' I protested.

**5** The cliffs were **a welcome** *vision/sight/show* after so many weeks at sea.

**6** He suffered a heart attack on stage, **in** *complete/open/full* **view of** the audience.

**7** I picked up the shiny stone to **take a** *handier/tighter/closer* **look**.

**8** For most of this week the comet will be **visible with the** *naked/bare/open* **eye**.

**9** Could you *keep/put/set* **your eye on** my bag, please? I'm just going to the toilet.

**10** We scanned the night sky, hoping to *give/catch/gain* **sight of** the comet.

### *Read* and *write*

1 Complete each of the phrasal verbs with an appropriate word from the box. In each section **1–4** the word required for both spaces is the same.

| up | into | off | out |
|---|---|---|---|

**1** I've just **written** _____ **to** the Polish Tourist Office **for** information on the Mazurian Lakes.
Western governments have come under increasing pressure to **write** _____ Third World **debts**.

**2** As soon as the interview was over, he **wrote** _____ **his notes** and faxed the report to his boss.
Contract law is a complex area, so it's wise to **read** _____ **on the subject** and take professional advice.

**3** She swallowed hard and **wrote** _____ **a cheque for** £4,560.
Let's hear what you've written for number 3. Can you **read** _____ **your answer**, please, Alex?

**4** The right to keep and bear arms is **written** _____ **the constitution** of the United States.
It's only an opinion poll – it would be wrong to **read too much** _____ **the results**.

2 Match each pair of definitions **a–d** to the appropriate pair of verbs in bold in exercise 1 above.

**a** include in (a law, contract or agreement); think something means more than it really does

**b** record in a full and complete form; read a lot about a subject in order to get information

**c** apply to an organization asking them to send something; cancel

**d** complete a printed document (eg prescription, receipt) with information; read aloud

**Self help**

Add the ***read* and *write*** expressions in bold in exercise 1 above to your vocabulary notebook, together with the definitions in exercise 2.

## Language focus

Grammar reference on page 223 of the Coursebook.

### Inversion

1 Complete each of the gaps with **one** word.

**Statement from the main opposition party**

At **(1)** _____ time in the last 60 years **(2)** _____ literacy levels in this country been so low. Not only **(3)** _____ the nation's teenagers reading less than ever before, **(4)** _____ many are also incapable of writing more than one sentence without making a spelling or punctuation mistake. **(5)** _____ since the 1940s have we witnessed such a decline in reading and writing standards.

**(6)** _____ no circumstances must this situation be permitted to continue. Only **(7)** _____ the government introduces a comprehensive reading programme for three to five-year-olds **(8)** _____ standards improve. **(9)** _____ then will the nation's youth be able to break free from the chains of illiteracy and recover its dignity. **(10)** _____ no account must we allow ourselves to be complacent; action must be taken now.

2 Complete each sentence with a suitable phrase. There is an example at the beginning **(0)**.

**0** Not for one moment ___*did we suspect*___ that David had stolen it – it took us all completely by surprise.

**1** No sooner ________________ home than my mother phoned.

**2** Only when ________________ the news on television did she realize the full scale of the tragedy.

**3** Never before in all my working life ________________ such an incompetent boss.

**4** Not until you've tidied your room ________________ you to go out and play with your friends!

**5** Hardly ________________ his new job when the company ran into problems and made him redundant.

**6** At no point in the marathon ________________ of giving up: I had promised myself I would finish it.

**7** Never again ________________ her advice – I'm in more trouble now than I was before.

**8** Little ________________ that someone was recording their conversation.

# Use of English

CAE Part 4

## Gapped sentences

For questions **1–5** below, think of **one** word only which can be used appropriately in all three sentences. In this exercise, the words required can be found in the reading text on pages 142 and 143 of the Coursebook. Here is an example **(0)**.

**0** We have suffered the worst floods on ___*record*___ this year, even worse than the floods in 1995.

There was so little traffic this morning that I got to work in ___*record*___ time.

I looked through Emma's old ___*record*___ collection to see if we'd listened to the same music as teenagers.

**1** Dangerous drivers do not have the slightest __________ for anyone else on the road.

Some of our staff have expressed __________ over the poor lighting in the office.

My personal life doesn't __________ you so please stop asking me about it.

**2** Explaining why the soldiers were sent in so quickly, an army spokesman said that the situation had __________ for immediate action.

The police were __________ to deal with the fight but no arrests were made.

The performance had to be __________ off after fire destroyed the stage.

**3** Jenny's boss asked her to give the team a brief __________ of what she'd seen at the exhibition.

When booking your holiday, please take into __________ the fact that cancellations are charged at 10%.

Do not leave your company laptop in your car on any __________.

**4** Our charity raises money for the homeless and for people in __________ in the inner city.

People __________ to be made aware of the additives that certain food contains.

We have no __________ of these toys now that our children have grown up.

**5** The restaurant was once famous for its __________ food and wine before it started serving burgers.

We walked on through the __________ rain, slowly but surely becoming soaking wet.

Despite his long flight, Eric said he felt __________ and would be present at the meeting.

CAE Part 3

## Word formation

For questions **1–10**, read the text below. Use the word given in capitals at the end of some of the lines to form a word that fits in the gap **in the same line**. There is an example at the beginning **(0)**.

### A COUNTRY AND WESTERN DEGREE

| | |
|---|---|
| Lyrics from country and western songs have **(0)** *enabled* a student | **ABLE** |
| to obtain a degree in geography and **(1)** ________ management. Sally | **ENVIRONMENT** |
| Hill, who **(2)** ________ in cultural and social geography during her | **SPECIAL** |
| three-year course, analysed in **(3)** ________ over 50 country songs as | **DEEP** |
| part of a study of the changing nature of relationships. According to Sally, | |
| the lyrics provide a fascinating **(4)** ________ into the way women's | **SIGHT** |
| **(5)** ________ of men have evolved. From the 1970s she used material | **PERCEIVE** |
| by Tammy Wynette, including *Run Woman Run*, a song **(6)** ________ | **WRITE** |
| from the point of view of an older woman **(7)** ________ a younger | **ADVICE** |
| woman to return to the man she has left, as she 'may not find true love | |
| again.' From the 1990s she quotes Shania Twain, who, in *Man, I Feel* | |
| *Like a Woman*, **(8)** ________ women to 'have a little fun' and 'go | **COURAGE** |
| totally crazy'. Sally says the **(9)** ________ for her idea came from her | **INPIRE** |
| mother, a fan of country music who describes herself as 'a fiercely | |
| **(10)** ________ and happily divorced woman'. | **DEPEND** |

CAE Part 1

## Multiple-choice cloze

For questions **1–12**, read the text below and decide which answer **(A, B, C** or **D)** best fits each gap. There is an example at the beginning **(0)**.

### Opera for everyone

You could be forgiven for **(0)** ________ the Royal Opera House (ROH) more with the over-50s than with the under-15s. But if you did, **(1)** ________ you might be surprised to learn that the ROH's education department reaches out every year to **(2)** ________ the young generation with opera. It is, however, safe to assume that opera can be an unfamiliar **(3)** ________ to most schoolchildren, and the first reaction **(4)** ________ by the ROH in the classroom is often bemusement. 'Children **(5)** ________ positively as long as you introduce them to opera in the right way,' explains Paul Reeve, the ROH's director of education. 'The older students can initially have an extreme negative reaction, but that **(6)** ________ is a great challenge. We give those **(7)** ________ kids the opportunity to experience what it's like to be, say, a composer or a choreographer, and that shows them the skill that is **(8)** ________ in the artforms.' One popular programme the ROH **(9)** ________ annually is *Write an Opera* and this year children from 28 UK schools will perform their work on stage in July. Teachers have found that while such a programme gives their pupils a greater **(10)** ________ of the arts, they have a broader effect, too. 'I don't think arts participation has an actual **(11)** ________ on developing people's creativity and self-esteem,' says Reeve, 'but the feedback we get is that participation in an opera project can have a hugely positive effect on children who have previously **(12)** ________ elsewhere in their school life.'

| | | | | |
|---|---|---|---|---|
| **0** | **A** tying | **B** relating | **C** joining | **D** associating |
| **1** | **A** then | **B** so | **C** even | **D** while |
| **2** | **A** reveal | **B** keep | **C** engage | **D** maintain |
| **3** | **A** way | **B** medium | **C** channel | **D** means |
| **4** | **A** developed | **B** projected | **C** provided | **D** encountered |
| **5** | **A** respond | **B** manage | **C** answer | **D** learn |
| **6** | **A** refusal | **B** resistance | **C** indifference | **D** disillusionment |
| **7** | **A** ironic | **B** doubtful | **C** sceptical | **D** improbable |
| **8** | **A** requested | **B** contained | **C** involved | **D** included |
| **9** | **A** sets up | **B** runs out | **C** comes up | **D** takes up |
| **10** | **A** fascination | **B** impression | **C** information | **D** awareness |
| **11** | **A** restriction | **B** monopoly | **C** control | **D** design |
| **12** | **A** performed | **B** focused | **C** struggled | **D** achieved |

## Writing

CAE Part 2

### Information sheet

1 Read the following extract from an information sheet, which was written for students in their final year at college. Write each of these section headings in an appropriate gap **a–c**.

The day of the interview Practice makes perfect Do your homework

# How to prepare for job interviews

*You've been invited for interview and now you want to make sure you do everything within your power to get the job. So what do you need to do to prepare yourself for the big day?*

**a)** ______________________________

**(0)** *Firstly, you should* find out as much as you possibly can about the position, the company, the industry and even the interviewer. **(1)** *You should go to* your prospective employer's website on the Internet, where the company presents itself as it wants to be seen; relevant trade journals will then tell you how it is viewed by others. **(2)** *You should perhaps also* speak to people who work or have worked for the company, if at all possible.

All this information will give you a great deal to talk about during the interview and so help create the right impression. The more you know, the greater your competitive edge over other candidates.

**b)** ______________________________

To help increase confidence, many people practise the interview in front of a mirror. However, **(3)** *you should instead* try it out with a real person: it's much more realistic and it gives you the chance to ask him or her for some feedback on your performance.

**(4)** *In particular, you should practise* answers to common questions you can expect to be asked. These include:

- What do you consider to be your major strengths and weaknesses?
- Why do you want to work for this company?
- Where do you see yourself in five years' time?

An interview is also your chance to decide whether you want to work for the company, so be prepared to ask three or four relevant questions yourself.

**c)** ______________________________

**(5)** *You shouldn't ever* underestimate the effect of your appearance on the interviewer: make sure you wear a suit to the interview, even if the normal working environment of the company allows for more informal dress. Punctuality is another crucial factor with regards to first impressions, and for this reason **(6)** *you should always* arrive at the interview site at least 15 minutes before your scheduled meeting.

*All that's left now is the interview itself!*
*See over for information and advice on successful interview strategies.*

2 Some information sheets may require you simply to explain facts or describe a procedure. The information sheet above, however, also gives advice, most of which is introduced with *you should* or *you shouldn't*.
It is important in your own writing to include a range of language. Replace each of the numbered phrases **1–6** in the information sheet with one of the expressions in the box. Write each expression in the appropriate space below. There is an example at the beginning **(0)**.

| | | |
|---|---|---|
| it's always wise to | it would be a mistake to | make a special point of rehearsing |
| ~~the first step is to~~ | it's far more advisable to | it's also worthwhile to |
| the best place to look is | | |

**0** *The first step is to*

**1** ______________ **4** ______________

**2** ______________ **5** ______________

**3** ______________ **6** ______________

3 Read the following Writing Part 2 task and do the activities in **A** and **B** below.

Some members of your English class recently commented that they would like to have had more advice at the beginning of the course on how to prepare for the CAE examination. You have agreed to write an information sheet giving a number of ideas and practical tips for future students to read at the start of their CAE exam preparation course.

Write the **text for the information sheet** in **220–260** words.

## A Gathering ideas

i The comments in **1–5** below were all made by students preparing to take the CAE examination. For each one decide which of the following aspects of English the student is focusing on. Each student may be focusing on more than one aspect.

| | | |
|---|---|---|
| Reading | Listening | Writing |
| Speaking | Vocabulary | Grammar |

**1** ______________

'Before my lesson on Friday each week, I always spend about an hour in the library doing a Paper 4 test from a past paper – with the headphones on, of course!'

**2** ______________

'I have two notebooks, one of which I use exclusively for recording new language and structures. In order for it to be a useful reference, I make sure I update and organize it on a regular basis.'

**3** ______________

'I've been visiting the website of an English language newspaper every week, looking at articles which interest me and noting down collocations which I think I might be able to use myself.'

**4** ______________

'It's the Part 1 compulsory question I find the most difficult, especially reports. I'm very busy at work, but I do try and make time to do all the homework my teacher sets for this particular paper – with my effort and her corrections I feel I'm really making progress.'

**5** ______________

'I get together with one of my classmates each week and we spend about an hour comparing and contrasting magazine photos or discussing a range of issues from money to marriage to mobile phones.'

ii If possible, add one further idea for each of the different aspects of English mentioned in exercise 1. Would you add any advice which does not fall into these categories?

## B Organizing ideas

As in the example on page 90, you might choose to divide your information sheet into three main sections. Which of the following groups of section headings **a–c** would be inappropriate when answering the task above?

**a**
**1** Receptive skills
**2** Productive skills
**3** Examination skills

**b**
**1** Revising what you have studied
**2** Making the most of your time during the exam
**3** Life after the CAE exam

**c**
**1** Using the coursebook
**2** Preparing with other students
**3** Preparing by oneself

4 Now write your answer to the task.

### How to go about it

- Organize your ideas from A into relevant sections. You may decide to use one of the appropriate groups of headings in B, or else use your own section headings.
- Decide on an appropriate register for your information sheet.
- Write your answer to the task using some of the advice language from exercise 2. Don't forget to include a brief introduction and ending.

# 12 The world about us

## Reading

CAE Part 2

### Gapped text

1 You are going to read an extract from a magazine article about an attempt to film hippos. Six paragraphs have been removed from the extract. Choose from the paragraphs **A–G** the one that fits each gap **(1–6)**. There is one extra paragraph which you do not need to use.

## Hippo Heaven

*What happens to a hippo when it sinks beneath the surface? Mzima was the place to find out.*

If there's a 'must-see' for a freshwater naturalist in East Africa, then it's *Mzima Spring* in Kenya's *Tsavo West National Park*. I first became aware of it as a teenager, when I was enthralled by Alan and Joan Root's classic film *Mzima: Portrait of a Spring*, with its extraordinary, underwater images of hippos. Back then I would have assumed that there were other sites like it, scattered throughout the continent.

1 ______

I therefore counted myself fortunate when my partner Vicky and I eventually got the chance to visit *Mzima* itself with Alan Root. It was the dry season, and as Alan flew us over *Tsavo* I was looking forward to seeing *Mzima* for the first time. But when Alan dipped a wing, I was totally unprepared for what leapt out of the monochrome scorched plains.

2 ______

I knew immediately that we had to make a film there and we believed that if we lived at *Mzima* for long enough then something incredible would reveal itself. Our goal was to film the behaviour of hippos under water to get some key sequences about which a story could be told. This meant either diving with them so frequently that we gained their trust or filming them unobserved from an underwater hide.

3 ______

So, after two weeks, we had only spent a total of thirty minutes underwater with no film and one attack to show for it. The chance of spending the thousands of hours underwater that we would normally do when making a film looked slim. Hippos are potentially more dangerous than crocodiles, but, the more we explored the spring, the more numerous the crocodiles we found – and the bolder they became.

4 ______

At the same time as trying to film underwater, we erected towers to give us an aerial view of the spring. From these, we could watch an entire group of hippos and look down through the water. What we saw was exciting. Female hippos were defending their young against crocodiles, but most extraordinary of all, we could see the hippos opening their mouths and having their teeth cleaned by *Labeo* fish, which swarmed inside their gaping jaws.

5 ______

The first time I tried it, this latest hide was secreted in the shallows, in the shade of an overhanging fig tree. I was in there waiting for the hippos to come close, when a troop of baboons arrived to investigate and discovered that the tree was in fruit. As they fed, figs started to rain down from above.

6 ______

At first it wasn't too bad but then the baboons realized that the best figs were in the branches directly above me. All this eating made them thirsty so they descended for a drink before carrying on with the feast. By the time Vicky came to relieve me, this had been going for several hours and the hippos had fled. There was only one thing for it; we would have to set about filming remotely. We ended up with a camera fixed to the bed of the spring and it took nine more months for the hippos to get used to that!

**A** I knew only too well what was coming next, but I couldn't escape. The golden rule about hide work is always to have someone else with you when you get in and out; any disturbance is then associated with that person and not the hide. But on this occasion, I was alone.

**B** It rapidly became apparent that neither method was going to work. When we tried to get into the water, the hippos either charged or fled. Meanwhile the local crocodiles became curious, and on the second or third dive on my way to the hide, I had been forced to fend one off by vigorously hitting it on the head with the camera.

**C** We were determined to film this underwater, but progress was dismal. In an idea borrowed from Alan Root, our assistant Norbert Rottcher constructed a new sort of hide, a type of 'reverse aquarium', comprising a large metal 'coffin', open on top, with a glass front through which we could film and stay dry.

**D** This may be because hippos can't see particularly well underwater. They compensate for this by being sensitive to sound, including the high-pitched sound produced by the camera. Despite our efforts, we couldn't muffle it.

**E** Nestled beneath us was an oasis of liquid turquoise, set in a ring of yellow fever trees. We circled, and each time we passed over, we could see the forms of hippos asleep in the pool. Through the crystal clear water, we could make out the green shapes of crocodiles and pale blue fish.

**F** With this in mind, we decided to build a tunnel of protective steel mesh to access the hide more safely. As a solution it seemed obvious, but the hippos found it obvious, too, and moved away. We then left the hide alone for several months, hoping that the hippos would get used to it, but for some reason, they never did.

**G** However, when I was filming hippos elsewhere in East Africa for a documentary twenty years later, I discovered that this was not the case.
The hippos were swimming in muddy water holes and coffee-coloured rivers, so no matter how exciting the behaviour visible above the surface, every time a hippo's nostrils pinched together, I knew my subject was about to disappear from view.

2 The following words are all used to describe *water* in the text:

*a* ***fresh****water naturalist*     ***crystal clear*** *water*     ***muddy*** *water holes*

Complete each of the gaps below with an appropriate word from the box. The words are all collocates of *water*.

| | | | | | | |
|---|---|---|---|---|---|---|
| flood | rain | salt | tap | drinking | running | sparkling |

**1** **A** 'We'd like to drink water with our meal, please.'
**B** 'Certainly, Madam. **Bottled** or __________ **water**?'
**A** 'Bottled, please.'
**B** 'And would you prefer **still** or __________ **water**?'

**2** Don't fill your bottles up from that tap – it's not safe __________ **water**.

**3** We collect __________ **water** in a large tank on the roof, then use it for things like watering the garden or cleaning the car.

**4** The merganser is a species of duck which can be seen on either **fresh** or __________ **water**, depending on the time of year.

**5** He lives in a house with no electricity, no gas and no __________ **water**.

**6** The basement was filled with __________ **water** after a night of torrential rain.

## Self help

Add the collocates of **water** to your vocabulary notebook.

# Vocabulary

Wordlist on page 215 of the Coursebook.

## Verb and noun collocations

1 One of the items of vocabulary in each group is not normally used with the verb in bold. Cross out the item which does not fit. There is an example at the beginning **(0)**.

| | | | | |
|---|---|---|---|---|
| **0 lead** | a race | to problems | a life | ~~the truth~~ |
| **1 meet** | a deadline | with success | hidden treasure | expectations |
| **2 make** | trouble | it to a meeting | housework | up one's mind |
| **3 welcome** | a decision | someone a favour | an opportunity | comments |
| **4 keep** | a promise | one's temper | a secret | an effort |
| **5 pay** | a lie | attention | a compliment | a bill |
| **6 wish someone** | luck | harm | birth | every happiness |

2 Complete the gaps with a verb and noun collocation from exercise 1. Write the appropriate form of the verb. There is an example at the beginning **(0)**.

**0** We got lost on the way, but we still *made* it to the *meeting* on time.

**1** Stop talking and ___________ ___________ !

**2** Tom certainly ___________ his ___________ to take care of my bicycle; in fact, it's in better condition now than when I lent it to him.

**3** Environmentalists have ___________ the Government's ___________ to abandon its controversial nuclear power programme.

**4** We ___________ you no ___________ : we come in peace.

**5** I eat the right food, I do regular exercise, I don't smoke; all in all I think I ___________ a reasonably healthy ___________ .

**6** They were disappointed with the restaurant: the food was reasonable, but the service failed to ___________ their ___________ .

**7** It was wrong to shout at him like that; you should have ___________ your ___________ and told him calmly that his behaviour was unacceptable.

**8** He failed to ___________ the 10 o'clock ___________ set by the newspaper, and his article was not published.

**9** I'm not sure whether to study chemistry or biology at university; I haven't ___________ up my ___________ yet.

**10** I've got my maths exam tomorrow – ___________ me ___________ !

## Approximation

Underline the correct alternative.

**1** The company produces *just/such/something* like 2,000 tons of the stuff every day.

**2** He should be out of hospital in a week or *approximately/about/so*.

**3** *Extremely/Very/Quite* nearly 85% of those surveyed said they were in favour of the proposal.

**4** *Just/Some/Few* under 3% said they were undecided.

**5** I reckon we'll get there *so/something/round* about 6 o'clock, don't you?

**6** It's a very exclusive area, with houses costing *upwards/more/over* of £750,000.

**7** They estimate there were *many/some/plenty* two and a half million people at the demonstration; that's over half the population of the entire city.

**8** She probably earns *something/round/upwards* in the region of £80,000 a year.

# Language focus

Grammar reference on page 224 of the Coursebook.

## Conjunctions

Rewrite each of the sentences using the word given. There is an example at the beginning **(0)**.

**0** She wore dark glasses because she didn't want to be recognized. (**so that**)
*She wore dark glasses so that she wouldn't be recognized.*

**1** I don't like boxing, but I still enjoyed the film *Ali*. (**even**)
______________________________

**2** Two of their players were sent off, but they still won the game. (**despite**)
______________________________

**3** If we don't phone her, she'll worry about us. (**otherwise**)
______________________________

**4** It doesn't matter how I comb it, my hair always looks a mess! (**however**)
______________________________

**5** You might want some more later, so I'll leave the plate there. (**in case**)
______________________________

**6** We spoke very quietly because we didn't want to wake my dad up. (**so as**)
______________________________

## Modal verbs

For questions **1–8** below, use the information in **a** to complete the gap in **b**, which is more formal. Choose from the words in the box. There is an example at the beginning **(0)**.

| | | | | |
|---|---|---|---|---|
| obliged | obligatory | ~~obligation~~ | permitted | forbidden |
| recommended | supposed | required | presumed | |

**0 a** We don't have to give the money back.
**b** We are under no *obligation* to refund the money.

**1 a** You mustn't smoke anywhere in the building.
**b** Smoking is not __________ in any part of the building.

**2 a** They've been told they mustn't speak to the press.
**b** They have been __________ to speak to the press.

**3 a** You really should wear strong shoes.
**b** Sturdy footwear is strongly __________ .

**4 a** You needn't pay until the course finishes.
**b** Payment is not __________ until the end of the course.

**5 a** Don't feel you have to give anything.
**b** You should not feel __________ to contribute.

**6 a** It should have got here a couple of weeks ago.
**b** It was __________ to arrive a fortnight ago.

**7 a** They think he must have left the country.
**b** He is __________ to have left the country.

**8 a** You must wear a seat belt.
**b** The wearing of seat belts is __________ .

# Use of English

## CAE Part 3

### Word formation

For questions **1–10**, use the word given in capitals at the end of some of the lines to form a word that fits in the gap **in the same line**. There is an example at the beginning **(0)**.

### Rainforest Concern

Frustrated and tired of hearing about the **(0)** *disappearing* rainforests? Well here's your chance to do something positive about it. **APPEAR**

The world's rainforests represent a vast reservoir of **(1)** ________ and hold potential for **KNOW**
the **(2)** _______ of new medicines and foods. There is no doubt that large-scale **DISCOVER**
deforestation alters the climate: it **(3)** _______ droughts in the dry season and floods in **INTENSE**
the rainy season. The result is fewer animal and plant species, soil **(4)** _______, a water **ERODE**
supply which is **(5)** _______ and poorer health for the local people. By joining Rainforest **RELY**
Concern and sponsoring acres of **(6)** _______ rainforest for the Choco-Andean Rainforest **THREAT**
Corridor in Ecuador, you will be protecting one of the world's most important **(7)** _______ **ECOLOGY**
areas. Within these forests live a high number of seriously **(8)** _______ species of animals, **DANGER**
birds and plants, many of which are found nowhere else on earth. You will also be helping
to secure the **(9)** _______ and culture of the Awa and Cayapas indigenous people, who still **SURVIVE**
live in harmony with their natural environment.

Please help this dynamic conservation project by completing the coupon now. Your
**(10)** _______ will be a wonderful gift for your children and for the Earth itself. For more details **SPONSOR**
on this and other projects, visit our website www.rainforestconcern.org.

## CAE Part 2

### Open cloze

For questions **1–15**, read the text below and think of the word which best fits each gap. Use only **one** word in each gap. There is an example at the beginning **(0)**.

### Life After Man: A vision of the Future

What if, overnight, humans **(0)** *were* wiped off the face of the Earth? Luckily for the world after humans, **(1)** ________ all the big mammals would be gone. A continent-sized museum, Africa, still holds **(2)** _________ is a striking collection. Would they spread **(3)** ______ the planet after we're gone? Could they replace the creatures we finished off elsewhere, or even evolve **(4)** ________ they finally resembled those same lost creatures? If **(5)** ________ were no people left, Africa, **(6)** __________ has been occupied by humans longer than **(7)** _________ other place, would paradoxically revert **(8)** ________ the purest primeval state on Earth. **(9)** ________ so much wildlife grazing and browsing, Africa is the **(10)** ________ continent where exotic plants haven't escaped suburban gardens to usurp the countryside. But Africa, **(11)** ________ the extinction of people, would include some key changes. For a start, North African cattle were once wild, **(12)** _________ after thousands of years with humans, they've been cross-bred to develop huge stomachs. This is **(13)** _________ they can eat huge amounts during the day, because it's too dangerous to graze at night. Consequently, they're not very quick. Left on their own, **(14)** __________ the protection of humans, they'd be rather vulnerable. And as cattle now account for more than half **(15)** ________ live weight of African savanna ecosystems, they would provide a feast for lions and hyenas. Once cows were gone, there would be more than double the feed for everything else.

CAE Part 4

## Gapped sentences

For questions **1–5** below, think of **one** word only which can be used appropriately in all three sentences. In this exercise, the words required can be found in the reading text on pages 155 and 156 of the Coursebook. Here is an example **(0)**.

**0** The moonlight revealed a strange _figure_ walking slowly towards the house.

We need to _figure_ out how to raise enough money to rebuild the damaged classroom.

Before we sign the contract, we need a precise _figure_ for the final cost and not an estimate.

**1** Emma likes to ________________ attention to herself by changing her hair colour every week.

The aim of the report is to ________________ a comparison between the effects of poverty on children living in rural and urban areas.

I heard the taxi ________________ up outside my house and knew my father had come home at last.

**2** I really dislike the way that our manager is always taking ________________ for everyone else's hard work.

I am still waiting for the bank to ________________ my account for the fees they overcharged me.

Once I finish this course, it will count as one ________________ towards my degree.

**3** Half the staff in our office have ________________ down with flu so the rest of us are doing overtime.

Her style of writing means that her characters ________________ to life on the very first page.

For teenagers buying clothes, style tends to ________________ before comfort.

**4** Paul is still upset about losing his job so you'll need to ________________ the subject carefully.

The government needs a new ________________ to tackling gun crime as their current policy isn't working.

With the ________________ of summer, I noticed the mornings grow lighter and my mood change for the better.

**5** If I've read the map correctly, this road should ________________ us back to town.

Akiko is auditioning to play one of the ________________ roles in this year's production of *Romeo and Juliet*.

If you're not sure about table manners in other countries, just follow your host's ________________ and you won't cause offence.

CAE Part 5

## Key word transformations

For questions **1–8**, complete the second sentence so that it has a similar meaning to the first sentence, using the word given. **Do not change the word given**. Use between **three** and **six** words, including the word given. Here is an example **(0)**.

**0** I'm sure a burglar came into our house while we were sleeping and stole the jewellery then.

**BROKEN**

Someone _must have broken into_ the house while we were sleeping and stolen the jewellery then.

**1** At Jeremy's leaving party, his boss made a speech and said he hoped Jeremy would have a good future.

**BEST**

At Jeremy's leaving party, his boss made a speech and wished ________________ the future.

2 Our attempts to persuade Soji to continue his studies weren't successful and he left university early.

**MET**

Our attempts to persuade Soji not to give ________________ no success and he left university early.

3 The interviewer told Belinda that he would write to her to inform her whether her application had been successful.

**KNOW**

The interviewer told Belinda that he would ________________ writing whether her application had been successful or not.

4 It's possible that the shops will sell all their bottled water so we should buy all we need now.

**CASE**

We should buy all the bottled water we need now ________________ out of it.

5 If we don't stop the sale of tiger products now, it's possible there will be no more tigers left within the next ten years.

**OTHERWISE**

We need to stop the sale of tiger products now ________________ out within the next ten years.

6 Even though Diego didn't know any French at all, he managed to communicate with the Parisian taxi driver.

**SINGLE**

Despite ________________ French, Diego managed to communicate with the Parisian taxi driver.

7 Tom's tutor told him that more effort was required in order to pass the course.

**MADE**

Tom's tutor told him he would fail the course ________________ effort.

8 I wish I hadn't let Max borrow my money because none of his investments has shown a profit.

**NEVER**

I ought ________________ my money to Max because none of his investments has shown a profit.

# Writing

CAE Part 2

## Proposal

1 Read the following Writing Part 2 task, then complete each of the gaps in the model answer with one of the words or expressions from the box. There is an example at the beginning **(0)**.

The local authority in the town where you are studying has announced its intention to increase the annual budget for environmental projects next year. As a member of a local environmental group you have been asked to submit a proposal for the authorities giving your suggestions. You should give details of how the money should be spent in at least **three** areas, including clear reasons for your recommendations.

Write your **proposal** in **220–260** words.

| | | | |
|---|---|---|---|
| therefore | instead | as | in order to |
| ~~the first of these~~ | this has led to | also | finally |
| whilst | clearly | as well as | |

## Recommendations for environmental projects for the town of Didcup

### Introduction

It is gratifying to observe that the local authority has decided to increase its financial commitment to environmental projects. There are three main areas requiring urgent attention and funding.

### Reducing Pollution

**(0)** *The first of these* is the unacceptably high level of pollution caused by exhaust fumes from cars and lorries. **(1)** _________ a higher incidence of respiratory illness among local inhabitants and a decline in the number of tourists visiting Didcup.

A substantial proportion of the budget should **(2)** _________ be allocated to the creation of more pedestrianized areas within the main shopping district. Money might **(3)** _________ be spent on an awareness raising campaign, encouraging people to leave their cars at home and use public transport **(4)** _________ .

### Green Areas

**(5)** _________ Didcup boasts a number of parks and gardens, there is a noticeable lack of trees, bushes and flowers on the pavements of our residential areas. **(6)** _________ the obvious aesthetic benefits of these plants to the town, they would release more oxygen into the atmosphere and help in the fight against pollution. **(7)** _________ , funds would also need to be set aside for the maintenance of these areas.

### Wildlife Protection

**(8)** _________ , some of the budget should be devoted to the preservation of the town's wildlife. Especially at risk are hedgehogs, hundreds of which are killed each year by traffic. **(9)** _________ protect these highly vulnerable animals, traffic signs could be erected warning drivers to look out for them. This would greatly benefit our gardens **(10)** _________ hedgehogs help control unwanted slugs and snails.

Indeed, all of these measures will make Didcup a much better place for everyone, whether they are resident or tourist, human or animal.

2 In the box below write those expressions from the model which refer to spending or using money.

*increased its financial commitment to*

3 **Either** write your own answer to the task in exercise 1

**or** write one of the following proposals.

**1** The principal of your college has been given a budget for the improvement of the learning environment in your college. Write a proposal for your principal, giving details of how the money should be spent in at least **three** areas and including clear reasons for your recommendations.

**2** Your manager at work has been given a budget for the improvement of the working environment in your branch or department. Write a proposal for your manager, giving details of how the money should be spent in at least **three** areas and including clear reasons for your recommendations.

### Don't forget!

- Plan your answer carefully.
- As in the model, use a range of vocabulary, structures and linking expressions.
- Write between 220–260 words.

# 13 Food for thought

## Reading

CAE Part 2

### Gapped text

1 You are going to read an extract from a magazine article about the history of the baguette, a kind of French bread. Choose from the paragraphs **A–G** the one that fits each gap **(1–6)**. There is one extra paragraph which you do not need to use.

## Give them stick

*Steven Kaplan, an American no less, is weaning the French off the travesty of a baguette they have eaten since 1945. John Lichfield reports*

You have to be a brave man to mess with a national symbol, especially someone else's national symbol. Steven Kaplan is not just brave, he is heroic. This week, Kaplan, an American, will publish the first gourmet guide to the baguettes of Paris. In Britain, the cliché Frenchman is a grumpy man wearing a beret, gripping a baguette under his arm. In France, the cliché Englishman is a mild man in a bowler with an umbrella over his arm. Like the bowler, the beret has become virtually extinct.

| 1 | |
|---|---|

Kaplan, a professor of European history, and one of the foremost authorities on the history of bread, calls it something else: 'an impostor, a tasteless, aroma-less monstrosity, which has existed for only half a century'. The real French baguette, whose history Kaplan has traced back to the 17th century, began to disappear after the Second World War. Bakers, even small, artisanal bakers, started to adopt modern methods which spawned feather-light, lily-white loaves.

| 2 | |
|---|---|

By the 1980s, the pre-war baguette, made from double-fermented dough, with no artificial yeast and no chemical additives, had almost gone the way of berets and other French exceptions. It took a campaign by *Real Bread* enthusiasts, including Kaplan, to prod the French government into promoting a retro-baguette revival. In six out of 10 Paris bakeries, the light, white 'standard baguette' is now sold alongside the succulent, longer-lasting, crunchy baguettes which used to exist in France.

| 3 | |
|---|---|

After careful consideration of appearance, smell and taste, he has made his choice and come up with a scoring system to grade quality using wheat-sheaves instead of stars. He has awarded 'three wheat-sheaves' to the best dozen; two to another 18 and one to the rest. Parisian bakers await his book with excitement and foreboding for Kaplan is not just an academic expert: he is a connoisseur, a man who trained as a baker, a man whose opinions are respected, even feared, throughout the French bread-making world.

| 4 | |
|---|---|

Kaplan judges baguettes in three ways. A good, traditional baguette should look lumpy and individual, not uniform. Inside, there should be a jumble of uneven holes in the bread. 'Smelling the bread, I want my nose to be assaulted by a wide and rich variety of aromas. If that's not there, I know that this is a mediocre baguette.' The taste of a good baguette should be a balance of sweet and sour, he says. It should 'both linger and alter in the mouth.'

| 5 | |
|---|---|

As it happens, part of Kaplan's motivation for writing the book is trying to invent a language in which to describe bread. 'We have specific descriptions for wine but not for bread, which is a more important, part of our civilisation. I wanted to try to create a vocabulary for bread which would be supple, and not too pompous.'

| 6 | |
|---|---|

Kaplan hopes his book will lay a trail of crumbs to lead Parisians back on to the path of the true taste of French bread. He prefers not to divulge, pre-publication, the names of all the 'three wheatsheaves' winners but we can be fairly certain that these may eventually become as prized as three *Michelin stars*.

**A** They are not the only ones. On the left bank of the city, where two of the capital's best, small bakers, Eric Kayser and Dominique Saibron do business, the conclusions are awaited with some anxiety. 'They are bitter rivals,' Kaplan says. 'but both make superb traditional baguettes.'

**B** It is this baguette, as defined rigorously by law in France since 1993, which is the principal subject of Kaplan's book *Cherchez le Pain*. Kaplan has eaten his way in the past eight months through 637 of Paris's 1,240 small bakeries testing this traditional bread. Against all expectations, he remains a very trim man.

**C** Celebrating, and encouraging, the revival of the old-style baguette is the other thing that drives him. In the general run of Parisian bakeries, the traditional baguette now represents 18 per cent of the turnover in baguettes. In other words, the fluffy, tasteless, white baguette, and its bigger sister, the 'pain', still rule the French table.

**D** But in fact Kaplan doesn't stop here. He speaks fluent French and often resorts to French words even to describe the texture of bread. His final pronouncement is that the bread beyond the crust should be '*moelleux*'. The wonderfully evocative word has no easy English translation; it means, roughly speaking, moist, soft and velvety.

**E** The baguette, however, thrives. Or does it? Anywhere in France, you can buy long tubes of fluffy, ultra-white dough, which will set into solid blocks within half a day. The world, including France, refers to this as a baguette or typical 'French loaf'.

**F** It is impossible to predict how they will react to his conclusions. 'The bad news is that half of small bakeries in Paris are producing traditional baguettes which are, quite frankly, awful,' says Kaplan. 'The good news is that even these bad, traditional baguettes are a hundred times better than standard, white baguettes.'

**G** The French were more than delighted with this. After the dark, indigestible bread they'd been forced to endure, the whiter-than-white loaf was very much welcome. It was a fresh start, a symbol of modernity.

2 Use the word given in capitals at the end of each sentence to form a noun that fits in the gap in that sentence. All the nouns you require appeared in the reading text. There is an example at the beginning **(0)**.

| | | |
|---|---|---|
| **0** | She could not hide her *excitement* at the prospect of working with the Australian superstar. | **EXCITE** |
| **1** | The traditional baguette is currently enjoying a _________ in France. | **REVIVE** |
| **2** | The book is beautifully illustrated and contains detailed _________ of the most common of our garden birds. | **DESCRIBE** |
| **3** | Children and adults alike are eagerly awaiting the ______ of the next book in the series. | **PUBLISH** |
| **4** | The government has yet to make an official _________ on the issue. | **PRONOUNCE** |
| **5** | Against all _________ , she reached the final of the competition. | **EXPECT** |
| **6** | The company has an annual _________ of £25 million. | **TURN** |
| **7** | The steam engine was lovingly restored by a group of railway _________ . | **ENTHUSIASM** |
| **8** | He awaited the results of the medical examination with a certain amount of _________ . | **ANXIOUS** |

# Vocabulary

Wordlist on page 215 of the Coursebook.

## Phrasal verbs and prepositions

In **A** and **B** below, complete each of the gaps with one of the prepositions from the relevant box. There is an example at the beginning **(0)**.

### A Eating and drinking

| | | | | |
|---|---|---|---|---|
| at | off | down | up | ~~up~~ |

**0** She heated *up* some of the previous day's stew in the microwave.
**1** I polished _____ the remains of that chocolate cake when I got home last night – I was so hungry!
**2** When he noticed the time, he gulped _____ the rest of his tea and hurried out.
**3** She sat at the table looking sad and dejected, just picking _____ her food.
**4** I often go for a run in the morning to work _____ an appetite for breakfast.

### B Deception

| | | | |
|---|---|---|---|
| at | for | into | on |

**1** He was tricked _____ signing the document, which effectively handed over possession of his house to his nephew.
**2** Let's play a trick _____ Stuart – we'll hide all his shoes in the washing machine!
**3** My brother confessed to me that he used to cheat _____ cards when we were younger.
**4** They've promised us a salary increase if we agree to work overtime, but we're not falling _____ their tricks any more – we know what they're up to.

## Expressions with *eat*

1 Complete each of the expressions in bold by writing an appropriate noun in each gap.

| | | | | | |
|---|---|---|---|---|---|
| bird | hand | home | horse | profits | words |

**1** When my son and his family come to stay they usually **eat us out of house and** _________ : it costs us a small fortune!
**2** Judy, our accountant, **has got** the boss **eating out of her** _________ : she can get him to do anything she wants.
**3** The increase in shoplifting from the company's city centre stores has **eaten into its** _________ quite considerably.
**4** I always said he'd be a failure, but I was **made to eat my** _________ recently when I read he'd become a millionaire three times over.
**5** Is dinner nearly ready? I **could eat a** _________ !
**6** I don't know how that child puts on weight – she **eats like a** _________ .

2 Match each of the expressions in **1–6** of exercise 1 with an appropriate meaning **a–e**.

***Example***: 1 c

**a** make someone like you so much they do whatever you want
**b** be forced to admit you were wrong about something
**c** eat a lot of someone's food when you are a guest in their home
**d** eat very little
**e** be extremely hungry
**f** use up or reduce a part of something, especially time or money

### Intensifiers

Match each sentence beginning **1–8** with an appropriate ending **a–h**.

1 All the flights to Manchester were **fully**
2 His new film is a convincing and **deeply**
3 The weather suddenly turned **bitterly**
4 My teenage son is a proud and **fiercely**
5 Prof. Amalric has written several **highly**
6 He's slowly recovering and **desperately**
7 Her next opponent is the **comparatively**
8 The long, hot walk left us feeling **utterly**

a **keen** to get back to work.
b **booked**, so we flew to Heathrow instead.
c **exhausted**, and we all went straight to bed.
d **influential** scientific papers on the subject.
e **moving** tale of one man's battle with alcoholism.
f **cold**, thanks to a chill wind coming from the east.
g **unknown** Pat Dale, who has yet to win a championship.
h **independent** child, but he still likes a cuddle from his mum.

**Self help**

Study the adverb + adjective collocations in bold in the exercise above for one minute. Then cover the sentence endings a–f and look only at the beginnings 1–6. How many collocations can you remember?

## Language focus

Grammar reference on page 225 of the Coursebook.

### Comparisons

In each of the following sentences one of the words is incorrect. Find the word and change it. There is an example at the beginning **(0)**.

**0** The food wasn't quite as spicy as I'd been told it might be and overall I enjoyed the meal, as ~~had~~ *did* everyone else in my family.

**1** By far the dullest job I've ever had was when I worked like a security guard in a high street clothes shop in Macclesfield.

**2** It wasn't so much Ralph's good looks which appealed to Eleanor and attracted her to him than his warm effervescent personality.

**3** Everyone said the listening exam was much more difficult than they thought it would be, but I didn't think it was anywhere close as hard as the ones we'd done in class.

**4** I much prefer our local supermarket to any of those huge out-of-town hypermarkets: apart from being a great amount more convenient, it's quite a lot cheaper, too.

**5** I can't understand why the film was such hugely successful: it wasn't nearly as good as his last one, yet it made five times as much at the box office.

**6** The more freedom you give children and the fewer limits you impose on them, the more unruly they become, in much the same way that certain types of plant, which will overrun a garden if they are not regularly cut back and held in check.

# Use of English

CAE Part 1

## Multiple-choice cloze

For questions **1–12**, read the text below and then decide which answer **(A, B, C** or **D)** best fits each gap. There is an example at the beginning **(0)**.

### The ready meal capital of Europe

In recent years, ready-made meals have **(0)** ______ Britain's eating **(1)** ______. Britons now spend four times as **(2)** ______ as the Italians on ready-made meals and six times more than the Spanish. Demand for instant meals has increased across Europe as a **(3)** ______, but why has Britain become the **(4)** ______ European capital of ready-made food, second only in the world to America?

Convenience is **(5)** ______ of the attraction. A recent survey **(6)** ______ that 77 per cent of purchasers said they only bought ready meals when they did not have time to cook. Dr Susan Jebb, head of nutrition at the Medical Research Council, said: 'People in the UK work the **(7)** ______ hours, we are very time-poor, and we don't have a strong cultural history of cooking.'

The ready-made meal boom also reflects changing social **(8)** ______ in Britain. More people live alone and so are less likely to be **(9)** ______ to cook. And with families eating together less often, ready meals allow people to eat what they want when they want. Julia Michna, of Marks and Spencer, says that ready meals also reflect changing **(10)** ______ in food. 'Britain's multiculturalism has brought a **(11)** ______ range of restaurants than other European countries, and ethnic cuisines, which people are often scared of cooking from scratch, are **(12)** ______ more popular. One quarter of chilled meals are Indian, and nearly one in five is Chinese.'

| | | | |
|---|---|---|---|
| **0 A** amended | **B** adjusted | **C** transferred | **D** <u>transformed</u> |
| **1 A** ways | **B** forms | **C** habits | **D** terms |
| **2 A** equal | **B** same | **C** much | **D** more |
| **3 A** conclusion | **B** total | **C** sum | **D** whole |
| **4 A** unclaimed | **B** unclassified | **C** undefeated | **D** undisputed |
| **5 A** element | **B** piece | **C** part | **D** share |
| **6 A** found | **B** made | **C** put | **D** gave |
| **7 A** hardest | **B** longest | **C** widest | **D** largest |
| **8 A** trends | **B** flows | **C** drifts | **D** movements |
| **9 A** convinced | **B** bothered | **C** worried | **D** disturbed |
| **10 A** desires | **B** likings | **C** tastes | **D** wishes |
| **11 A** longer | **B** deeper | **C** harder | **D** wider |
| **12 A** very | **B** quite | **C** far | **D** such |

CAE Part 2

## Open cloze

For questions **1–15**, read the text below and think of the word which best fits each gap. Use only **one** word in each gap. There is an example at the beginning **(0)**.

### Distraction burglaries

**(0)** *An* estimated 3,000 highly mobile criminals are earning **(1)** _____ to £40 million a year by robbing and tricking elderly people **(2)** _____ of cash, in many cases their life savings. Some 300,000 pensioners are falling victim **(3)** _____ 'distraction burglaries' each year, say police. Three quarters of victims are women, **(4)** _____ an average age of 81. Nine out of 10 victims live alone.

Many victims feel **(5)** _____ have been complicit in some ways by letting the thieves trick their way **(6)** _____ their homes and keep quiet about losing money or property, believing relatives may prevent **(7)** _____ living on their own. Crimes range from simple distraction of the victim by one thief – possibly posing **(8)** _____ a policeman or gas or electricity worker, **(9)** _____ others burgle a house – to the extortion of large amounts of money for poor quality work on houses or gardens.

The scale of distraction burglaries **(10)** _____ only emerged recently. Around 16,000 such offences are recorded in England and Wales each year. Thieves will travel hundreds **(11)** _____ miles in a day to find victims and to avoid police. They often operate as families, using children **(12)** _____ young as six to distract victims, for example by kicking a ball into their garden. Profits **(13)** _____ thought to be considerable: one family of thieves was found **(14)** _____ have £3.5 million in assets, with **(15)** _____ sign of legitimate employment whatsoever.

CAE Part 3

## Word formation

For questions **1–10** read the text below. Use the word given in capitals at the end of some of the lines to form a word that fits in the gap **in the same line**. There is an example at the beginning **(0)**.

### Don't forget!

- Look at the words before and after each space to help you choose the correct part of speech.
- You may need to use the negative or plural form of a noun.
- You may need to use the negative form of an adjective or adverb.

### A Vegetarian Cookbook

| | |
|---|---|
| If you often have **(0)** *difficulty* knowing what to serve for a mixed | **DIFFICULT** |
| **(1)** ________ of vegetarians and non-vegetarians, *Vegetarian Dishes for All* | **GATHER** |
| is a definite must-have. Its **(2)**________ range of mouth-watering soups, | **IMAGINE** |
| starters, salads, pasta dishes, gratins and desserts provides ample | |
| **(3)** ________ to the most sceptical of meat-eaters that vegetarian food is | **PROVE** |
| not automatically dull in flavour or **(4)** ________ in appearance. The recipes, | **ATTRACT** |
| which are **(5)** ________ straightforward, will teach both the novice and the | **REFRESH** |
| expert how to cook vegetables **(6)** ________ and with spectacular results. | **CREATE** |
| Easy-to-find ingredients are used in a wide range of inspiring **(7)** ________, | **COMBINE** |
| which will delight every one of your guests, and elevate your cooking skills | |
| to new **(8)** ________. There's also a special chapter for parents, with an | **HIGH** |
| impressive and tasty selection of recipes aimed at **(9)** ________ even the | **COURAGE** |
| **(10)** ________ of young eaters to meet their daily requirement of vegetables. | **FUSS** |

CAE Part 4

## Gapped sentences

For questions **1–5**, think of **one** word only which can be used appropriately in all three sentences. In this exercise, the words required are from the reading extracts on pages 172 and 173 of the Coursebook. Here is an example **(0)**.

**0** The company has announced that it may have to ___lay___ off workers or relocate them to other factories.

I'm sure Martin will try to ___lay___ the blame on someone else for his mistake.

We ___lay___ flowers on my grandfather's grave every year.

**1** Don't show that huge spider to Miranda or you'll probably __________ her to death!

The rise in violent crime in our capital is likely to __________ away tourists.

There was another bomb __________ in the business district yesterday and we all had to leave our offices.

**2** Their new __________ of clothing is meant to appeal to a younger target group.

There was no point in shooting at the wolf as it was already out of __________.

Prices at the store __________ from the easily affordable to the extremely expensive.

**3** Many children __________ hungry when their family is affected by long-term unemployment.

I've been in the same kind of job for years and I'd like to have a __________ at something new.

That beef will quickly __________ off in this heat unless you put it in the fridge.

**4** Please __________this email to anyone in the department who would benefit from a training weekend.

Let's sit further __________ so we can get a better view of the play.

A bit more __________ planning would have prevented our staffing problem.

**5** Could you __________ for me and answer the phone while I'm out of the office?

The book has an unimaginative __________ which does not make you want to pick it up.

The detectives were working under __________ to expose the gang leader.

# Writing

CAE Part 1

## Article

Read the following Writing Part 1 task.

You are the Secretary of the English Club at your school. The Director of Studies has written to you about an evening spent recently by the club at a local restaurant. Read the extract from her email, together with the advertisement and the notes you have made, and write an article for the school magazine telling students about the evening and encouraging them to participate in future club dinners.

> I'd like the dinner to become a regular event, and an article about the first one would be a great advertisement. The turnout was good, but the more students we can get to come in future, the better.
>
> Thanks
>
> Maria
>
> PS Mention some of the topics people spoke about – really interesting!

**The English Club**
***invites you to its first***
**Club Dinner**

7.30pm on Tuesday, November 11th
at the Cosmopolitan Restaurant

Speak English with teachers and other students as you enjoy a three-course meal in relaxed surroundings. Whatever your level, it'll be a great way to meet others and practise your English!

*Notes:*
- *teachers and other students* – *and the waiters and waitresses!*
- *three-course meal* – *brilliant food – for example ...*
- *Whatever your level* – *a good mixture there*

Write your **article** in **180–220** words.

**Don't forget!**

- Underline key words in the question to ensure you answer it correctly.
- Expand on one or two of the points in the input material, adding relevant information of your own.

# 14 Money matters

## Reading

CAE Part 1

### Multiple choice

1 You are going to read three extracts which are all concerned in some way with giving and receiving money. For questions **1–6**, choose the answer **(A, B, C** or **D)** which you think fits best according to the text.

### What's so good about Educational Maintenance Allowance?

Education Maintenance Allowance (EMA) could give you up to £30 a week to help out with the costs of staying in learning after 16. The money's paid directly into your bank account. Once it's there, you can use it to pay for whatever you like – for example, books, travel or equipment. Whatever you learn after 16, it could be your springboard to getting good training, better qualifications, a decent job and higher pay later on, too. Experts have predicted that within three years, fewer jobs will be open to people without at least five good General Certificate in Secondary Education results, or the equivalent (such as a National Vocational Qualification level 2). So the more qualifications you get, the more choice and earning potential you'll have in return.

Furthermore, you won't have to stop working part-time if you get EMA, and your earnings won't make any difference at all to how much EMA you can get. EMA will also not affect any other benefits that you or your parents receive. If you qualify, EMA payments are £10, £20 or £30 per week, depending on your household income. You could also get cash bonuses if you do well on your course, and meet targets set by your school, college or learning provider. To get EMA, you must be aged 16, 17 or 18, and about to leave, or have already left, compulsory education. You must also be thinking about starting one of the following types of learning programme in England: a full-time further education course at college or school or a course that leads to an Apprenticeship.

**1** What are we told about the EMA in the first paragraph?
- **A** It must be paid back once a person is in full-time work.
- **B** There are certain restrictions on how it can be spent.
- **C** It can improve a person's chances of employment.
- **D** There is a limited period of time during which it is available.

**2** A young person's entitlement to EMA depends on
- **A** their continuing residence in the parental home.
- **B** the kind of education programme they plan to take.
- **C** the income they receive from their own job.
- **D** their level of performance on their course.

### Extract from a newspaper article

My experience of pretending to be a homeless person gets tougher as the day wears on. People are extraordinarily kind to me but their generosity seems to dwindle as my need increases. Early on, when I looked like a nice presentable kid, people gave to me easily. The wide community of the middle class looks after its own, it appears. But it's much harder to get people's attention now that I look bedraggled and slightly desperate. It's early evening when I enter *Pizza Express* and offer to wash dishes in return for garlic bread. The manager pats me on the back. 'Margherita pizza OK for you?' He says: 'You're young, things are hard in London.' I'm stunned by his kindness. He hands me a warm takeaway box which I scamper off with. I approach a real tramp and invite him to share the pizza.

With his second bite he asks loudly 'And to drink?' and bursts into laughter. I laugh too. It's the best pizza I've ever tasted.

It's getting late now, and the streets are deserted. I feel daunted by the long journey home. It's 10pm and I have a growing sense of panic. I have no money for transport. Drunk people laugh at me and I feel vulnerable. I want to call after them 'I'm really one of you!' Eventually, I crawl on the back of a bus and plead with the conductor – something I swore I'd never do, because it puts him in such a difficult position. I feel immoral and degraded. I stumble home about midnight. My feet don't heal for a week. In the final hour, I've had a glimpse of what it might really be like to have no money. Absolutely horrible.

**3** In the first paragraph, what point is made about acts of charity?
- **A** Giving money is not always the most useful form of charity.
- **B** People on low incomes are more generous than wealthier people.
- **C** It is better to find a way to help yourself than depend on charity.
- **D** People donate money to others they have something in common with.

**4** The writer suggests she is reluctant to take a bus because she
- **A** is alarmed by other passengers.
- **B** is worried she will be recognized.
- **C** feels guilty towards the conductor.
- **D** is genuinely poor.

## Latest research into charitable spending

Two economists and a cognitive psychologist have studied how the brain reacts when people are given money to 'spend' – on both a food aid project and government taxes. As the volunteers in the study watched a series of computerized financial transactions take place, a brain scanner analysed which deep-seated parts of the brain were stimulated. Nerve cells in the *caudate nucleus* and the *nucleus accumbens* parts of the brain normally fire when someone eats a favourite food. This time they became excited when the money went to a food charity – but less so when it went to a tax office. 'The surprising element for us was that in a situation in which your money is simply given to others – where you do not have a free choice – you still get reward-centre activity,' said Professor Ulrich Mayr, a psychologist at the University of Oregon. 'I don't think that most economists would have suspected that.'

Mayr goes on to say that this explains the warm glow people report they experience from the act of charitable giving and reinforces the idea that there is true altruism. 'I've heard people claim that they don't mind paying taxes, if it's for a good cause – and here we showed that you can actually see this reaction going on inside the brain, and even line 26
measure it,' he said. However, he warned that society could not rely on people to give voluntarily because some people were prepared to take a 'free ride' on others' charitable donations.

**5** The findings of the study reveal that people
- **A** would prefer to avoid paying money to the government.
- **B** feel positive when their money is given to charity.
- **C** want to know exactly how their taxes are spent.
- **D** have different spending patterns to what economists believe.

**6** Which phrase is echoed by the words 'this reaction' in line 26?
- **A** warm glow
- **B** true altruism
- **C** good cause
- **D** free ride

2 **a** Underline the following verbs in the second extract.

| |
|---|
| dwindle |
| pat |
| scamper |
| plead |
| stumble |

**b** Use context to help you match the verbs in 2**a** to the definitions **a–e** below.

- **a** move quickly with small light steps ____________
- **b** move with difficulty and nearly fall because you are tired or ill ____________
- **c** become less over a period of time until almost nothing remains ____________
- **d** ask for something in an urgent or emotional way ____________
- **e** touch someone gently several times with a flat hand ____________

# Vocabulary

Wordlist on page 215 of the Coursebook.

## Money

Complete each of the gaps with one of the words from the box.

| | | |
|---|---|---|
| redundancy | counterfeit | sponsorship |
| pocket | ransom | housekeeping |

**1** Several members of a criminal gang have been arrested on charges of printing and passing _________ **money**.

**2** Some parents give their children far too much _________ **money** each week.

**3** She could never afford to buy meat or fish because her husband used to spend half the _________ **money** in the pub on Friday night.

**4** The kidnappers released the hostages two hours after the _________ **money** was paid.

**5** The factory where he worked was forced to close down and he used some of his _________ **money** to pay off his mortgage.

**6** I swam 163 lengths of the pool non-stop and raised over £500 in _________ **money**, which I donated to a local hospital.

## Verbs usually associated with money

1 For questions **1–5**, underline the correct verb **A**, **B**, **C** or **D**.

**1** The discovery of a second set of fingerprints _________ **weight to the theory** that Brooks did not act alone.
**A** owes **B** pays **C** lends **D** invests

**2** The Minister _________ **tribute to** rescue workers for their 'courage in the face of adversity'.
**A** sold **B** paid **C** lent **D** spent

**3** I know a quicker way to get there if you want to _________ **some time**.
**A** invest **B** spend **C** save **D** borrow

**4** The French writer _________ **the idea** for his first novel **from** an old Russian folk tale.
**A** borrowed **B** bought **C** saved **D** charged

**5** The company _________ **its success** to the quality of its products.
**A** pays **B** lends **C** sells **D** owes

2 Which of the correct verbs in exercise 1 collocates with each group of nouns?

**1** _________ a compliment/attention/one's respects

**2** _________ a favour/an apology/an explanation

**3** _________ support/credibility/assistance

**4** _________ effort/energy

**5** _________ a word/a phrase

### Self help

Add the **Verbs usually associated with money** to your vocabulary notebook, together with the nouns which collocate with them.

3 Complete the gaps using appropriate verb and noun collocations from exercise 2. Write the correct form of the verb, and if necessary, use an article (*a/an*) with the noun. There is an example at the beginning **(0)**.

**0** I didn't really hear what he said; I wasn't _paying_ much _attention_, to be honest.

**1** It seems I _______ you _______ ; I doubted your honesty, and clearly I was wrong. I hope you can forgive me.

**2** Over a hundred people came to the funeral to _______ their last _______ to the woman who had done so much for the local community.

**3** In order to refer to the first night of a film or a play, English has _______ the French _______ 'premiere', meaning 'first'.

**4** I had to help him, really – I felt I _______ him _______ for that time he fixed my car for me.

**5** When I said your new hairstyle was 'different', it wasn't a criticism: on the contrary, I was _______ you _______ .

## Language focus

Grammar reference on page 225 of the Coursebook.

### Noun phrases

1 Complete each of the gaps with one of the words from the box.

| | | | | |
|---|---|---|---|---|
| chances | depths | height | matter | grain |
| sense | sign | source | state | pack |

**1** I keep forgetting people's names; I think it must be **a** _________ **of age**.

**2** It's not exactly **a** _________ **of life and death**, but I would appreciate it if you could get it done as soon as possible.

**3** There wasn't **a** _________ **of truth** in what he said – his speech was **a** _________ **of lies** from start to finish.

**4** I felt **an** enormous _________ **of relief** when I heard I'd passed.

**5** After the rioting, the government declared **a** _________ **of emergency**, calling out the troops and imposing a night-time curfew.

**6** I have no investments or savings, so the state pension is my only _________ **of income**.

**7** Whether you're in **the** _________ **of winter** or **the** _________ **of summer**, AirFlow® ensures the temperature inside your home is exactly how you want it.

**8** The team's _________ **of promotion** to the First Division suffered a blow yesterday when they lost at home to relegation candidates Bristol City.

2 There is one mistake in each of the following sentences. Find the mistakes and correct them. There is an example at the beginning **(0)**.

**0** We had ~~lamb's~~ *lamb* chops for lunch yesterday.

**1** I'm going to get another beer can – I'm really thirsty.

**2** He tried to turn the handle of door, but realized he'd been locked in.

**3** She didn't have an evidence's scrap to support her accusations.

**4** She gave me several useful advice pieces on cooking with pastry.

**5** We had to write a three pages essay on the importance of money in today's society.

**6** The hotel could only guarantee him a week work.

**7** They gazed in wonder at the snow-covered mountains' tops.

**8** I read about it in last April edition of *Gardening Monthly*.

# Use of English

CAE Part 2

## Open cloze

For questions **1–15**, read the text below and think of the word which best fits each gap. Use only **one** word in each gap. There is an example at the beginning **(0)**.

### The sales

It is December. The first frost and snow of winter **(0)** *are* upon us and, as **(1)** ____ drawn by some mysterious force, otherwise sane, ordinary people are getting up at 5am **(2)** ____ queue for hours in the cold and dark. The sales have begun. Before Christmas!

As mere amateur bargain-hunters have always suspected, **(3)** ____ is a black art to sales shopping. Cunning sales veterans, determined to avoid the horrid changing-room queue, do their trying-on weeks **(4)** ____ advance. Then, **(5)** ____ the doors are flung open, they'll push, elbow and lock coat-hangers with **(6)** ____ another to reach the object **(7)** ____ their desire. This Darwinian struggle is carried **(8)** ____ in a terribly polite way, as everybody else pretends that everybody else **(9)** ____ being 'so pushy'. Their treasures clutched to their breast, their cheerfulness is barely disguised, in **(10)** ____ of the uncomfortable weight of armfuls of plates, dishes, sheets and towels.

The only shadow is the sight of other attractive bargains **(11)** ____ picked out by fellow shoppers.

People rarely do their sales shopping **(12)** ____ their own; it's mostly done in a threesome of mothers and daughters. They argue about skirt lengths and bathrobe colours, but **(13)** ____ shines through is a sense of unshakeable warmth, support and mutual understanding. The same is true **(14)** ____ men: they stand outside, holding bags and bonding in **(15)** ____ own 'What are we doing here?' way. Sales shopping certainly brings people together.

CAE Part 3

## Word formation

For questions **1–10**, read the text below. Use the word given in capitals at the end of some of the lines to form a word that fits in the gap **in the same line**. There is an example at the beginning **(0)**.

### Millionaire Cheat

| | |
|---|---|
| Three people who attempted to **(0)** *defraud* the television quiz show | **FRAUD** |
| *Who Wants to be a Millionaire?* have all been found guilty of **(1)** __________ | **DECEIVE** |
| at Southwark Crown Court. Major Charles Ingram appeared as a | |
| **(2)** __________ on the programme in September 2001, when, with the help | **CONTEST** |
| of his wife, Diana, and accomplice Tecwen Whittock, he won the top prize | |
| of £1 million. But his **(3)** __________ appearance was never broadcast and | **WIN** |
| the cheque was cancelled. Production staff called to the **(4)** __________ said | **TRY** |
| they grew suspicious of Ingram's **(5)** __________ hesitations and changes | **NUMBER** |
| of mind, and became aware of the **(6)** __________ coughing of a member of | **PERSIST** |
| the audience. Chris Tarrant, the show's host, noticed how Ingram often | |
| seemed **(7)** __________ about the answers he gave. Whittock, a college | **SURE** |
| lecturer from Cardiff, coughed **(8)** __________ from his seat to indicate the | **STRATEGY** |
| correct answer as Ingram said the four alternatives to each question out loud. | |
| A video **(9)** __________ of the programme was played in court as part of the | **RECORD** |
| prosecution case. The defendants, who had denied all accusations of | |
| **(10)** __________, listened impassively as sentence was passed. | **HONEST** |

CAE Part 5

## Key word transformations

For questions **1–8**, complete the second sentence so that it has a similar meaning to the first sentence, using the word given. **Do not change the word given**. Use between **three** and **six** words, including the word given. Here is an example **(0)**.

**0** By closing down the second warehouse we can save money and save jobs.
**ENABLE**
Closing down the second warehouse _will enable us to cut_ costs and save jobs.

**1** We would like you to pay for the delivery of this special order before you receive it.
**IF**
We would appreciate ________________ advance for the delivery of this special order.

**2** Scientists think that there is nothing on that planet to suggest there is any life there.
**SIGN**
According to scientists, there appears ________________ life on that planet.

**3** When I caught my boyfriend reading my emails, I told him I felt he had invaded my privacy.
**AN**
When I caught my boyfriend reading my emails, I told him I regarded it ________________ my privacy.

**4** It is now 24 hours since Mr William's boat sank and people think there is little likelihood he will survive.
**CHANCES**
It is now 24 hours since Mr Williams's boat sank and his ________________ to be slim.

**5** I regret not having the feeling of achieving anything after reaching the summit but I was too exhausted.
**SENSE**
I wish I ________________________ after reaching the summit but I was too exhausted.

**6** Jane really wants to have everyone looking at her every time we go out in a group.
**BE**
Jane can't help __________________ attention every time we go out in a group.

**7** I hoped to persuade the boss of the benefit to me of going away on a camping trip for ten days.
**WOULD**
I hoped to persuade the boss that a __________________ me good.

**8** Although the job meant that he earned money regularly, Tony did not enjoy it.
**REGULAR**
Although the job provided him ________________ of income, Tony did not enjoy it.

## Writing

CAE Part 2

Read the Paper 2 Writing tasks below. Before you write your answer, read the *How to go about it box* and do the *Key vocabulary* exercises on page 115.

Choose **one** of the following writing tasks. Your answer should follow exactly the instructions given. Write **220–260** words.

**1** Your region has recently been affected by adverse weather conditions, which have caused a great deal of damage to property and agriculture, as well as disrupting services and communications. A friend of yours from abroad has written to you expressing concern after seeing television pictures of some of the damage. Write a **letter** to your friend to reassure him or her, describing what happened, how your region has been affected and what is being done to tackle the situation.

**2** You see this announcement in an English language magazine.

> **A place to live in**
>
> We'd like to hear how readers feel about the village, town or city where they are currently living. How satisfied are you and what would you change about it? Write and tell us about at least two changes you would make saying how the place would benefit from these changes and how they would affect you personally.

Write your **article** for the magazine.

**3** You are a member of a health and fitness club in the town where you live. You have been asked to produce an information sheet in English for new members from other countries. You should:

- inform new members about some of the facilities that are available.
- give advice on how to use these facilities safely.
- briefly explain the procedure to follow if an accident occurs.

Write the **information sheet**.

**4** You have recently had a class discussion on consumerism and the range of products available to consumers. Your teacher has asked you to write an essay, giving your opinion on the following statement.

*Consumers have too much choice.*

Write your **essay** in **220–260** words

### How to go about it

- Select your Part 2 task carefully. Consider, in particular, whether you will be able to demonstrate a good range of vocabulary and structures when answering the task. The *Key vocabulary* exercises are designed to give you some help with this important aspect of the task.
- Plan your answer carefully before writing it. Follow the checklist of points for planning and checking your work on page 193 of the Coursebook.

## Key vocabulary

### Task 1

1 Match each of the adjectives **1–5** with an appropriate noun **a–e**.

| | |
|---|---|
| **1** torrential | **a** flooding |
| **2** gale-force | **b** storm |
| **3** widespread | **c** rain |
| **4** a violent | **d** snow |
| **5** thick | **e** winds |

2 Complete each of the gaps with one of the nouns from the box.

Families
Power lines
Crops
Tiles
Roads

**1** __________ were blown off roofs by high winds.
**2** __________ were brought down by falling trees.
**3** __________ were flooded out of their homes.
**4** __________ were blocked by deep snow drifts.
**5** __________ were destroyed in farming areas.

### Task 2

Complete each of the gaps with one of the verbs from the box, then match each sentence beginning **1–5** with an appropriate ending **a–e**.

demolished
pedestrianized
built
installed
introduced

| | |
|---|---|
| **1** More street lighting should be __________ | **a** to keep the town's youth out of trouble. |
| **2** The shopping district should be __________ | **b** to increase security at night. |
| **3** The disused railway station should be __________ | **c** to improve transport links with the nearest town. |
| **4** A new sports centre should be __________ | **d** to make way for a children's playground. |
| **5** A more frequent bus service should be __________ | **e** to reduce traffic pollution in the town centre. |

### Task 3

Complete each of the gaps with one of the verbs from the box.

begin
maintain
spend
wait
warm

**1** Remember to __________ up first by doing stretching exercises.
**2** On no account should you __________ longer than fifteen minutes in the sauna.
**3** It is important that you __________ two hours after a meal before swimming.
**4** Be sure to __________ an upright posture on the rowing machine.
**5** When using the treadmill, it is always advisable to __________ on a slow setting.

### Task 4

Complete each of the gaps with one of the nouns from the box.

source
control
demand
life
debts

**1** Choice can improve our **quality of** _______.
**2** Having a wide range of products enables us to **exercise** _______ **over** what we consume.
**3** This leads many to overspend, sometimes **incurring substantial** _______.
**4** The realization that we cannot afford the best in the range can be a **major** _______ **of dissatisfaction**.
**5** Companies produce unnecessary goods in their attempt to **satisfy consumer** _______ **for** variety.

## Before you write

For more information and useful language for each of the tasks, consult the relevant pages in the Ready for Writing unit in the Coursebook.

# Word formation list

## Nouns

### *-age*

| Verb | Noun |
| --- | --- |
| break | breakage |
| cover | coverage |
| pack | package |
| post | postage |
| store | storage |
| wreck | wreckage |

| Adjective | Noun |
| --- | --- |
| short | shortage |

### *-al*

| Verb | Noun |
| --- | --- |
| (dis)approve | (dis)approval |
| arrive | arrival |
| bury | burial |
| deny | denial |
| dismiss | dismissal |
| propose | proposal |
| rehearse | rehearsal |
| remove | removal |
| renew | renewal |
| revive | revival |
| survive | survival |

### *-ance*

| Verb | Noun |
| --- | --- |
| annoy | annoyance |
| (dis)appear | (dis)appearance |
| attend | attendance |
| disturb | disturbance |
| endure | endurance |
| enter | entrance |
| ignore | ignorance |
| inherit | inheritance |
| perform | performance |
| rely | reliance |
| resemble | resemblance |
| resist | resistance |
| signify | (in)significance |
| tolerate | (in)tolerance |

| Adjective | Noun |
| --- | --- |
| arrogant | arrogance |
| distant | distance |
| (un)important | (un)importance |
| (ir)relevant | (ir)relevance |
| reluctant | reluctance |

### *-ence*

| Verb | Noun |
| --- | --- |
| confide | confidence |
| depend | (in)dependence |
| differ | difference |
| exist | existence |
| insist | insistence |
| obey | obedience |
| occur | occurrence |
| offend | offence |
| persist | persistence |
| recur | recurrence |

| Adjective | Noun |
| --- | --- |
| absent | absence |
| (in)competent | (in)competence |
| (in)convenient | (in)convenience |
| evident | evidence |
| innocent | innocence |
| intelligent | intelligence |
| (im)patient | (im)patience |
| present | presence |
| violent | violence |

### *-cy*

| Adjective | Noun |
| --- | --- |
| (in)accurate | (in)accuracy |
| (in)adequate | (in)adequacy |
| (in)decent | (in)decency |
| (in)efficient | (in)efficiency |
| (in)frequent | (in)frequency |
| immediate | immediacy |
| infant | infancy |
| intimate | intimacy |
| (il)literate | (il)literacy |
| pregnant | pregnancy |
| private | privacy |
| redundant | redundancy |
| secret | secrecy |
| urgent | urgency |
| vacant | vacancy |

## -dom

| Adjective | Noun |
|---|---|
| bored | boredom |
| free | freedom |
| wise | wisdom |

| Person | Abstract noun |
|---|---|
| king | kingdom |
| star | stardom |

## -ful

| Noun | Noun (Quantity) |
|---|---|
| arm | armful |
| cup | cupful |
| fist | fistful |
| hand | handful |
| house | houseful |
| room | roomful |
| spoon | spoonful |

## -hood

| Person | Abstract noun |
|---|---|
| adult | adulthood |
| child | childhood |
| father | fatherhood |
| man | manhood |
| mother | motherhood |
| neighbour | neighbourhood* |
| parent | parenthood |
| woman | womanhood |

*neighbourhood
part of a town or city where people live

| Adjective | Noun |
|---|---|
| likely | likelihood |

## -iety

| Adjective | Noun |
|---|---|
| anxious | anxiety |
| notorious | notoriety |
| sober | sobriety |
| various | variety |

## -ity

| Adjective | Noun |
|---|---|
| (un)able | (in)ability |
| (in)active | (in)activity |
| complex | complexity |
| credible | credibility |
| curious | curiosity |
| (un)equal | (in)equality |
| (un)familiar | (un)familiarity |
| ferocious | ferocity |
| (in)flexible | (in)flexibility |
| (in)formal | (in)formality |
| generous | generosity |
| hostile | hostility |
| immune | immunity |
| intense | intensity |
| major | majority |
| minor | minority |
| (im)mobile | (im)mobility |
| objective | objectivity |
| (un)original | (un)originality |
| personal | personality |
| (un)popular | (un)popularity |
| prosperous | prosperity |
| (im)pure | (im)purity |
| (in)secure | (in)security |
| (in)sensitive | (in)sensitivity |
| severe | severity |
| similar | similarity |
| simple | simplicity |
| (in)sincere | (in)sincerity |
| stupid | stupidity |
| subjective | subjectivity |
| (in)valid | (in)validity |

## -ing

| Verb | Noun |
|---|---|
| advertise | advertising |
| build | building |
| gather | gathering |
| like | liking |
| live | living |
| meet | meeting |
| record | recording |
| say | saying |
| set | setting |
| suffer | suffering |

## -ment

| Verb | Noun |
|---|---|
| achieve | achievement |
| (dis)agree | (dis)agreement |
| amaze | amazement |
| amuse | amusement |
| announce | announcement |
| argue | argument |
| arrange | arrangement |
| commit | commitment |
| content | contentment |
| develop | development |
| disappoint | disappointment |
| discourage | discouragement |
| embarrass | embarrassment |
| employ | (un)employment |
| encourage | encouragement |
| enjoy | enjoyment |
| entertain | entertainment |
| excite | excitement |
| govern | government |
| improve | improvement |
| invest | investment |
| involve | involvement |
| judge | judgement/judgment |
| manage | management |
| measure | measurement |
| move | movement |
| (re)pay | (re)payment |
| punish | punishment |
| refresh | refreshment |
| replace | replacement |
| require | requirement |
| retire | retirement |
| settle | settlement |
| treat | treatment |

## -ness

| Adjective | Noun |
|---|---|
| (un)aware | (un)awareness |
| careless | carelessness |
| close | closeness |
| (un)conscious | (un)consciousness |
| deaf | deafness |
| eager | eagerness |
| (in)effective | (in)effectiveness |
| (un)friendly | (un)friendliness |
| great | greatness |
| hard | hardness |
| hopeless | hopelessness |
| (un)selfish | (un)selfishness |
| serious | seriousness |
| stiff | stiffness |
| thorough | thoroughness |
| tired | tiredness |
| useful | usefulness |
| weak | weakness |

## -ship

| Person | Abstract noun |
|---|---|
| champion | championship |
| companion | companionship |
| friend | friendship |
| leader | leadership |
| member | membership |
| owner | ownership |
| partner | partnership |
| scholar | scholarship* |
| sponsor | sponsorship** |

*scholarship
money given to someone to help pay for their studies

**sponsorship
money given to someone/an organization to help pay for something, eg an event

| Adjective | Noun |
|---|---|
| hard | hardship |

## -sis

| Verb | Noun |
|---|---|
| diagnose | diagnosis |
| emphasize | emphasis |

## -sion

| Verb | Noun |
|---|---|
| collide | collision |
| convert | conversion |
| erode | erosion |
| exclude | exclusion |
| expand | expansion |
| include | inclusion |
| persuade | persuasion |
| supervise | supervision |

## -son

| Verb | Noun |
|---|---|
| compare | comparison |

## *-ation*

| Verb | Noun |
|---|---|
| adapt | adaptation |
| administer | administration |
| apply | application |
| combine | combination |
| compile | compilation |
| consider | consideration |
| expect | expectation |
| explain | explanation |
| identify | identification |
| imagine | imagination |
| inflame | inflammation |
| inform | information |
| inspire | inspiration |
| interpret | interpretation |
| observe | observation |
| prepare | preparation |
| present | presentation |
| publish | publication |
| (dis)qualify | (dis)qualification |
| realize | realization |
| resign | resignation |
| vary | variation |

## *-tion*

| Verb | Noun |
|---|---|
| accommodate | accommodation |
| (re)act | (re)action |
| associate | association |
| collect | collection |
| complicate | complication |
| compose | composition |
| (dis)connect | (dis)connection |
| contaminate | contamination |
| demonstrate | demonstration |
| direct | direction |
| evolve | evolution |
| hesitate | hesitation |
| imitate | imitation |
| inhibit | inhibition |
| investigate | investigation |
| (de)motivate | (de)motivation |
| operate | operation |
| perceive | perception |
| predict | prediction |
| prescribe | prescription |
| receive | reception |
| recognize | recognition |
| reduce | reduction |
| repeat | repetition |
| (dis)satisfy | (dis)satisfaction |
| (re)solve | (re)solution |
| subscribe | subscription |
| substitute | substitution |

## *-th*

| Adjective | Noun |
|---|---|
| broad | breadth |
| deep | depth |
| long | length |
| strong | strength |
| true | truth |
| warm | warmth |
| wide | width |
| young | youth |

| Verb | Noun |
|---|---|
| grow | growth |

## *-ure*

| Verb | Noun |
|---|---|
| close | closure |
| compose | composure |
| depart | departure |
| expose | exposure |
| fail | failure |
| please | pleasure |
| proceed | procedure |
| sign | signature |

## *-y*

| Adjective | Noun |
|---|---|
| difficult | difficulty |
| (dis)honest | (dis)honesty |
| poor | poverty |
| safe | safety |
| (un)certain | (un)certainty |

| Verb | Noun |
|---|---|
| discover | discovery |
| enter | entry |

# People

### -ant

| Verb | Person |
| --- | --- |
| apply | applicant |
| assist | assistant |
| confide | confidant(e) |
| consult | consultant |
| contest | contestant |
| defend | defendant |
| inhabit | inhabitant |
| occupy | occupant |
| participate | participant |

### -ar

| Verb | Person |
| --- | --- |
| lie | liar |

### -ative

| Verb | Person |
| --- | --- |
| represent | representative |

### -er

| Verb | Person |
| --- | --- |
| employ | employer |
| lecture | lecturer |
| manufacture | manufacturer |
| present | presenter |
| read | reader |
| research | researcher |
| win | winner |

### -ian

| Noun | Person |
| --- | --- |
| electricity | electrician |
| history | historian |
| library | librarian |
| mathematics | mathematician |
| music | musician |
| politics | politician |

### -ist

| Noun | Person |
| --- | --- |
| bicycle | cyclist |
| environment | environmentalist |
| motor (car) | motorist |
| nature | naturalist |
| novel | novelist |
| psychiatry | psychiatrist |
| science | scientist |
| specialism | specialist |
| violin | violinist |

### -or

| Verb | Person |
| --- | --- |
| act | actor |
| collect | collector |
| communicate | communicator |
| compete | competitor |
| conduct | conductor |
| contribute | contributor |
| demonstrate | demonstrator |
| distribute | distributor |
| instruct | instructor |
| invent | inventor |
| spectate | spectator |

# Nouns formed with *up, down, in, away, out, back*

### *up-*

upbringing
upkeep
uprising
uproar
upset
upturn

### *down-*

downfall
downpour
downside
downturn

### *-down*

breakdown

### *in-*

income
input
insight
intake

### *-away*

getaway
hideaway
runaway
takeaway

### *out-*

outbreak
outburst
outcome
outline
outlook
output
outset

### *-out*

breakout
checkout
handout
knockout
lookout
payout
turnout
workout

### *-back*

comeback
drawback
feedback
setback

### *back-*

background

# Miscellaneous

| Verb | Noun |
|---|---|
| (mis)behave | (mis)behaviour |
| choose | choice |
| complain | complaint |
| die | death |
| give | gift |
| know | knowledge |
| laugh | laughter |
| lose | loss |
| prove | proof |
| receive | receipt |
| respond | response |

| Verb | Noun |
|---|---|
| sell | sale(s) |
| succeed | success |
| think | thought |
| try | trial |
| weigh | weight |

| Adjective | Noun |
|---|---|
| high | height |

# Adjectives

## -able

| Verb | Adjective |
|---|---|
| accept | (un)acceptable |
| advise | (in)advisable |
| afford | affordable |
| agree | (dis)agreeable |
| apply | (in)applicable |
| appreciate | appreciable |
| approach | (un)approachable |
| avoid | (un)avoidable |
| bear | (un)bearable |
| believe | (un)believable |
| compare | (in)comparable |
| consider | (in)considerable |
| desire | (un)desirable |
| dispense | (in)dispensable |
| forget | (un)forgettable |
| imagine | (un)imaginable |
| irritate | irritable |
| note | notable |
| notice | noticeable |
| pay | payable |
| predict | (un)predictable |
| prefer | preferable |
| prevent | preventable |
| regret | regrettable |
| rely | (un)reliable |
| remark | (un)remarkable |
| respect | respectable |
| understand | understandable |
| work | (un)workable |

| Noun | Adjective |
|---|---|
| comfort | (un)comfortable |
| fashion | (un)fashionable |
| knowledge | knowledgeable |
| memory | (un)memorable |
| profit | (un)profitable |
| reason | (un)reasonable |
| value | valuable/invaluable* |

*invaluable:
extremely useful. eg *invaluable advice/experience/help*

## -ible

| Noun | Adjective |
|---|---|
| access | (in)accessible |
| flexibility | (in)flexible |
| sense | (in)sensible* |

| Verb | Adjective |
|---|---|
| comprehend | (in)comprehensible |
| respond | (ir)responsible |

* sensible:
showing or having good sense eg *Cycling with a broken arm is not a very sensible thing to do.*

insensible:
a unconscious
eg *He was found drunk and insensible.*
b not caring about or unaware of
eg *She seemed insensible to the dangers involved.*

## -al

| Noun | Adjective |
|---|---|
| accident | accidental |
| addition | additional |
| alphabet | alphabetical |
| behaviour | behavioural |
| centre | central |
| culture | cultural |
| ecology | ecological |
| emotion | (un)emotional |
| environment | environmental |
| exception | (un)exceptional |
| experiment | experimental |
| fact | factual |
| globe | global |
| intention | intentional |
| medicine | medicinal |
| method | methodical |
| monument | monumental |
| nation | national |
| occasion | occasional |
| occupation | occupational |
| origin | (un)original |
| parent | parental |
| person | (im)personal |
| practice | (im)practical |
| profession | (un)professional |
| sensation | (un)sensational |
| society | social |
| temperament | temperamental |
| tradition | traditional |
| universe | universal |

### -ial

| Noun | Adjective |
|---|---|
| benefit | beneficial |
| commerce | commercial |
| controversy | (un)controversial |
| face | facial |
| finance | financial |
| industry | industrial |
| influence | influential |
| manager | managerial |
| matrimony | matrimonial |
| residence | residential |
| secretary | secretarial |
| substance | (in)substantial |
| territory | territorial |

### -ant

| Verb | Adjective |
|---|---|
| ignore | ignorant |
| please | (un)pleasant |
| rely | reliant |
| resist | resistant |
| signify | (in)significant |
| tolerate | (in)tolerant |

### -ent

| Verb | Adjective |
|---|---|
| appear | apparent |
| confide | confident |
| depend | (in)dependent |
| differ | (in)different |
| insist | insistent |
| obey | (dis)obedient |
| persist | persistent |
| recur | recurrent |

| Noun | Adjective |
|---|---|
| absence | absent |
| (in)competence | (in)competent |
| (in)convenience | (in)convenient |
| evidence | evident |
| (in)frequency | (in)frequent |
| innocence | innocent |
| intelligence | intelligent |
| (im)patience | (im)patient |
| presence | present |
| violence | violent |

### -ate

| Noun | Adjective |
|---|---|
| accuracy | (in)accurate |
| adequacy | (in)adequate |
| appropriacy | (in)appropriate |
| consideration | (in)considerate |
| fortune | (un)fortunate |
| moderation | (im)moderate |

### -ative

| Verb | Adjective |
|---|---|
| administer | administrative |
| argue | argumentative |
| compare | comparative |
| consult | consultative |
| imagine | (un)imaginative |
| inform | (un)informative |
| prevent | preventative |
| provoke | provocative |
| represent | (un)representative |

## -ive

| Verb | Adjective |
|---|---|
| act | (in)active |
| adopt | adoptive |
| appreciate | (un)appreciative |
| assert | (un)assertive |
| attend | (in)attentive |
| attract | (un)attractive |
| communicate | (un)communicative |
| compete | (un)competitive |
| conclude | (in)conclusive |
| construct | (un)constructive |
| cooperate | (un)cooperative |
| create | (un)creative |
| deceive | deceptive |
| decide | (in)decisive |
| defend | defensive |
| describe | descriptive |
| destroy | destructive |
| disrupt | disruptive |
| divide | divisive |
| explode | explosive |
| express | expressive |
| extend | extensive |
| impress | (un)impressive |
| include | inclusive |
| invent | inventive |
| offend | (in)offensive |
| persuade | persuasive |
| possess | possessive |
| produce | (un)productive |
| progress | progressive |
| protect | protective |
| receive | (un)receptive |
| respect | (ir)respective |
| respond | (un)responsive |
| speculate | speculative |
| succeed | successive |
| support | (un)supportive |

| Noun | Adjective |
|---|---|
| aggression | (un)aggressive |
| effect | (in)effective |
| expense | (in)expensive |
| secret | secretive |
| sense | (in)sensitive |

## -ing/-ed

The following verbs can be used to form participle adjectives
eg *worrying/worried*

*alarm, amaze, amuse, annoy, astonish, bore, confuse, convince, depress, disappoint, disgust, embarrass, entertain, excite, exhaust, fascinate, frighten, frustrate, increase, interest, irritate, motivate, move, refresh, relax, satisfy, shock, surprise, terrify, threaten, thrill, tire, worry*

The following *-ing* adjectives are commonly used with the nouns in brackets.

| Verb | Adjective |
|---|---|
| close | closing (date) |
| consult | consulting (room) |
| recur | recurring (illness, nightmare, problem, theme) |
| run | running (water) |
| support | supporting (actor, actress, evidence, role) |

## -ous

| Noun | Adjective |
|---|---|
| (dis)advantage | (dis)advantageous |
| ambition | (un)ambitious |
| anxiety | anxious |
| caution | cautious |
| courtesy | (dis)courteous |
| curiosity | curious |
| danger | dangerous |
| disaster | disastrous |
| glamour | (un)glamorous |
| hazard | hazardous |
| humour | humorous |
| luxury | luxurious |
| monster | monstrous |
| mystery | mysterious |
| nerve | nervous |
| number | numerous |
| poison | poisonous |
| religion | (ir)religious |
| suspicion | suspicious |

| Verb | Adjective |
|---|---|
| infect | infectious |
| vary | various |

## *-ful/-less*

| Root | -ful | -less/un__ful |
|---|---|---|
| beauty | beautiful | ———— |
| care | careful | careless |
| cheer | cheerful | cheerless* |
| colour | colourful | colourless |
| count | ———— | countless |
| deceit | deceitful | ———— |
| delight | delightful | ———— |
| effort | ———— | effortless |
| end | ———— | endless |
| event | eventful | uneventful |
| faith | faithful | unfaithful |
| fault | faulty | faultless |
| flight | ———— | flightless |
| gratitude | grateful | ungrateful |
| hair | hairy | hairless |
| harm | harmful | harmless |
| heart | ———— | heartless |
| help | helpful | helpless*/unhelpful* |
| home | ———— | homeless |
| hope | hopeful | hopeless |
| job | ———— | jobless |
| meaning | meaningful | meaningless |
| pain | painful | painless |
| peace | peaceful | ———— |
| point | ———— | pointless |
| power | powerful | powerless |
| price | ———— | priceless* |
| relent | ———— | relentless |
| resource | resourceful | unresourceful |
| respect | respectful | disrespectful |
| skill | skilful*/skilled* | unskilled |
| sleep | ———— | sleepless |
| speech | ———— | speechless |
| stress | stressful | unstressful |
| success | successful | unsuccessful |
| taste | tasty*/tasteful* | tasteless |
| thought | thoughtful* | thoughtless |
| time | ———— | timeless |
| truth | truthful | untruthful |
| use | useful | useless |
| waste | wasteful | ———— |
| wonder | wonderful | ———— |
| worth | ———— | worthless* |
| youth | youthful | ———— |

**cheerless:** used mainly to describe the weather or a room which is not bright or pleasant

**helpless:** unable to do anything to help or protect yourself

**unhelpful:** not willing to help other people

**priceless:** used to describe an object which has a very high value; it is worth so much money that the price cannot be calculated (compare with *worthless* below)

**skilful & skilled:** both can be used to describe a person who has the necessary ability, experience and/or training to do something well.
*eg He's a skilful footballer. This work was done by skilled craftsmen.*

**skilled:** can also be used to describe a job or piece of work that requires special skill and training
*eg Nursing is a skilled job.*

**tasty:** used to describe food with a strong and pleasant flavour

**tasteful:** used to describe clothes, decoration etc which is attractive and shows good taste

**thoughtful:**
a to describe a person who is quiet and serious because they are thinking about something
b to describe someone who thinks and cares about the feelings and needs of other people

**worthless:** used to describe an object with no value in money (compare with *priceless* above)

## *-ic*

| Noun | Adjective |
|---|---|
| allergy | allergic |
| drama | dramatic |
| optimism | optimistic |
| pessimism | pessimistic |
| science | scientific |
| strategy | strategic |

### *-ary*

| Noun | Adjective |
| --- | --- |
| caution | cautionary |
| literature | literary |
| revolution | revolutionary |
| **Verb** | **Adjective** |
| imagine | imaginary |
| volunteer | (in)voluntary |

### *-ory*

| Verb | Adjective |
| --- | --- |
| advise | advisory |
| celebrate | celebratory |
| contradict | contradictory |
| explain | explanatory |
| introduce | introductory |
| migrate | migratory |
| oblige | obligatory |
| prepare | preparatory |
| satisfy | (un)satisfactory |
| supervise | supervisory |

### *-ly*

| Noun | Adjective |
| --- | --- |
| friend | (un)friendly |
| life | lively |
| time | (un)timely |

### *-y*

| Noun | Adjective |
| --- | --- |
| chat | chatty |
| cloud | cloudy |
| ease | easy |
| fault | faulty |
| fog | foggy |
| frost | frosty |
| grass | grassy |
| guilt | guilty |
| hair | hairy |
| hill | hilly |
| mist | misty |
| mud | muddy |
| rain | rainy |
| rock | rocky |
| sleep | sleepy |
| sun | sunny |
| wealth | wealthy |

## Verbs

### *-ate*

| Noun | Verb |
| --- | --- |
| alien | alienate |
| assassin | assassinate |
| difference | differentiate |
| value | evaluate |
| **Adjective** | **Verb** |
| active | activate |
| captive | captivate |
| dominant | dominate |
| valid | validate |

### *en-*

| Noun | Verb |
| --- | --- |
| act | enact |
| circle | encircle |
| courage | encourage (discourage) |
| danger | endanger |
| force | enforce |
| list | enlist |
| rage | enrage |
| trust | entrust |
| **Adjective** | **Verb** |
| able | enable |
| large | enlarge |
| rich | enrich |
| sure | ensure |

### *-ify*

| Noun | Verb |
| --- | --- |
| class | classify |
| example | exemplify |
| glory | glorify |
| identity | identify |
| note | notify |
| (dis)qualification | (dis)qualify |
| **Adjective** | **Verb** |
| clear | clarify |
| just | justify |
| pure | purify |
| simple | simplify |
| solid | solidify |

### *-en*

| Adjective | Verb |
|---|---|
| black | blacken |
| bright | brighten |
| broad | broaden |
| dark | darken |
| dead | deaden |
| deaf | deafen |
| deep | deepen |
| fat | fatten |
| flat | flatten |
| hard | harden |
| high | heighten |
| long | lengthen |
| less | lessen |
| loose | loosen |
| red | redden |
| sad | sadden |
| sharp | sharpen |
| short | shorten |
| soft | soften |
| stiff | stiffen |
| straight | straighten |
| strong | strengthen |
| sweet | sweeten |
| thick | thicken |
| tight | tighten |
| weak | weaken |
| wide | widen |
| worse | worsen |

| Noun | Verb |
|---|---|
| threat | threaten |

### *-ize*

| Noun | Verb |
|---|---|
| character | characterize |
| climate | acclimatize |
| computer | computerize |
| criticism | criticize |
| emphasis | emphasize |
| maximum | maximize |
| memory | memorize |
| minimum | minimize |
| moisture | moisturize |
| pressure | pressurize |
| revolution | revolutionize |
| standard | standardize |
| summary | summarize |
| symbol | symbolize |
| sympathy | sympathize |

| Adjective | Verb |
|---|---|
| commercial | commercialize |
| familiar | familiarize |
| formal | formalize |
| general | generalize |
| item | itemize |
| modern | modernize |
| social | socialize |
| special | specialize |
| stable | stabilize |
| visual | visualize |

## Verbs formed with *up, down, over, under, out*

### *up-*

update
upgrade
uphold
uplift
uproot
upset
upstage

### *down-*

downgrade
download
downplay
downshift
downsize

### *over-*

overcome
overcook
overeat
overestimate
overexpose
overflow
overhear
overheat
overload
overlook
overrate
overrule
overrun
overshadow
oversleep
overspend
overstay
overstretch
overtake
overthrow
overuse
overwork

## *under-*

underachieve
undercharge
undercut
underestimate
undergo
underline
underrate
understate
undertake
undervalue

## *out-*

outgrow
outlast
outlive
outnumber
outplay
outrun
outstay

# Unit 1

## Reading 1, page 4

### CAE Part 4 Multiple matching

**1** B

**2** **1** G **2** E **3** B **4** C **5** D **6** G
**7** B **8** D **9** A **10** B **11** C **12** E
**13** F **14** A **15** F

## Vocabulary, page 6

### Verb and noun collocations

| | |
|---|---|
| **1** into | **2** with |
| **3** out | **4** in |
| **5** to | |

### Adjective and noun collocations

**1**

| | |
|---|---|
| **1** inside | **2** resounding |
| **3** burning | **4** hard |
| **5** terrible | **6** urgent |
| **7** heated | **8** outlying |

**2**

| | |
|---|---|
| **1** slim | **2** recurrent |
| **3** daunting | **4** poor |
| **5** overnight | **6** dismal |
| **7** lifelong | **8** sporting |

### Word formation

| | |
|---|---|
| **1** exposure | **2** proposals |
| **3** inflexibility | **4** vacancies |
| **5** emphasis | **6** requirements |
| **7** closeness | **8** shortage |
| **9** irrelevance | **10** notoriety |

## Language focus, page 7

### Spelling

| Incorrect spelling | Correct spelling |
|---|---|
| writting | writing |
| apeared | appeared |
| Loosers | Losers |
| wich | which |
| agresive | aggressive |
| wellfare | welfare |
| totaly | totally |
| althought | although |
| their | there |
| ougth | ought |
| adition | addition |
| intervue | interview |
| where | were |
| oportunity | opportunity |
| impresive | impressive |
| pane | pain |
| too | to |
| extremly | extremely |
| innacuracies | inaccuracies |
| faithfuly | faithfully |

### Modal verbs: *might, could, may, can*

**1**

**1** live here, but we never see him
**2** (very) well be asked to speak French during the interview
**3** not have known you were married
**4** (well) have got it
**5** as well sell it
**6** have told me you were vegetarian
**7** have been enjoying herself very much

**2**

| | | | |
|---|---|---|---|
| **1** can | **2** could | **3** may | **4** could |
| **5** may | **6** could | **7** could | |

## Use of English, page 9

### CAE Part 1 Multiple-choice cloze

**1** B **2** D **3** D **4** C **5** A **6** B
**7** A **8** C **9** B **10** D **11** D **12** A

## Writing, page 10

### CAE Part 2 Competition entries

2 **C** Björn Borg

3 In the first paragraph the writer gives a general introduction to the person he/she is nominating. In the final paragraph the writer reiterates the case for the nomination and leaves the reader something to think about: *who knows what else he might have achieved.*

4 Borg's achievements are mainly described in paragraph 2.

The writer gives a number of reasons for the nomination: Borg was the most outstanding player of his generation; he achieved so much so young; unlike other players he remained calm under pressure; he had a strong influence on the way the game is played today; retiring early helped make him into a legend.

5 *one of the all-time greats; this highly talented young man, put all others in the shade; he outclassed all the other big names; what set him apart from these players was; at the height of his career.*

### Useful language

1 class
2 head
3 peak
4 ability
5 match
6 gift
7 none
8 standard

# Unit 2

## Reading, page 12

### CAE Part 3 Multiple choice

**1** A **2** A **3** D **4** C **5** D **6** B **7** A

## Vocabulary, page 14

### Changes

**1**

**1** transferred **2** shifted
**3** adapted **4** altered

**2**

**1** B **2** D **3** A **4** C **5** A

**3**

**1** scene **2** heart
**3** pace **4** direction
**5** fortunes **6** condition
**7** law **8** attitudes

## Language focus, page 15

**1**

**1** used to **2** was (still) eating
**3** met **4** have eaten
**5** have seen/saw **6** had caught
**7** have stayed **8** hadn't given
**9** have done **10** to sit

**2**

**A**

1 has been putting
2 has managed
3 has met
4 believed/used to believe
5 asked/used to ask/would ask
6 have changed
7 said
8 lit/used to light/would light

**B**

1 went
2 saw/had seen
3 was working/worked
4 booked/had booked
5 Having washed
6 had just landed
7 had been experiencing
8 would take/was going to take
9 spent
10 didn't arrive
11 had been sitting
12 had left/would be leaving/was going to leave/ was leaving
13 had ever had
14 would be/was going to be

## Use of English, page 16

### CAE Part 3 Word formation

**1** latest
**2** beautifully
**3** adaptation
**4** dissatisfaction
**5** starring
**6** sales
**7** variation
**8** discovery
**9** threatens
**10** historians

### CAE Part 4 Gapped sentences

**1** bring
**2** sides
**3** subject
**4** switch
**5** sweeping

### CAE Part 5 Key word transformations

**1** have warned/told you not to
**2** if/though Anita has (recently) been/begun/started
**3** didn't use to like/enjoy
**4** gone/been to see the apartment (for)
**5** would like to have carried/gone/continued
**6** like to express my dissatisfaction
**7** would sooner have stayed
**8** you rather I hadn't let

## Writing, page 18

### CAE Part 1 Formal and informal letters

**2**

**1** satisfaction
**2** deal
**3** knowledge
**4** explanations
**5** attention
**6** improve
**7** Firstly
**8** departure
**9** failed
**10** addition
**11** illness
**12** Finally
**13** discover/learn/hear
**14** arrival
**15** entrance/admission

# Unit 3

## Reading, page 20

### CAE Part 2 Gapped text

**1** = E **2** = A **3** = B **4** = C **5** = F **6** = D
G = not used

## Vocabulary, page 22

### Adjective and noun collocations

**1** *Across:* **3** ambition **5** aroma **6** method **8** success **11** change **12** challenge
*Down:* **1** changes **2** odour **4** information **7** failure **9** chance **10** smell

**2** *Possible answers (see also Wordlist on pages 209–211 of the Coursebook)*
lifelong/secret **ambition**
pleasant/sweet **aroma**
convenient/efficient **method**
huge/great **success**
refreshing/pleasant **change**
formidable/major **challenge**
far-reaching/significant **changes**
acrid/stale **odour**
biased/reliable **information**
total/continued **failure**
slight/remote **chance**
faint/rancid **smell**

### Verb and noun collocations

**1**

**2** an ambition
**3** information
**4** a challenge
**5** change
**6** a problem
**7** a possibility
**8** a smell

**2**

**2** pursue
**3** gathering
**4** presents
**5** resisting
**6** resolved
**7** looking into
**8** get rid of

### Word formation

**1** ignorant
**2** countless
**3** inaccessible
**4** numerous
**5** surprisingly
**6** literary
**7** unsuccessful
**8** comparative
**9** dramatically
**10** introductory

## Language focus, page 24

**1**

**1** had seen/watched
**2** rather/sooner have
**3** been for
**4** have worn/taken
**5** to have
**6** Had I
**7** you had, would/could have
**8** might/would not/never, been driving/travelling

**2**

| | |
|---|---|
| **1** C | **2** A, B, C |
| **3** B | **4** A, B, C |
| **5** A, B | **6** B, C |
| **7** C | **8** A, C |

## Use of English, page 25

**CAE Part 1 Multiple-choice cloze**

**1** D **2** C **3** C **4** B **5** B **6** D
**7** A **8** B **9** C **10** C **11** B **12** B

**CAE Part 4 Gapped sentences**

**1** steps
**2** stood
**3** care
**4** claim
**5** issues

## Writing, page 26

**CAE Part 1 Formal letters**

**A**

**2** is more appropriate: it summarizes the information from the survey as instructed, and focuses only on those aspects which are of most relevance to the task.
**1** merely copies the information from the survey, using the same words.

**B**

**1** Priority *more important to have a decent library*
**2** journey *too far for many*
**3** claim *nonsense!*
**4** evidence *where's the proof?*

**C** *Possible answers*

**1** the elderly, the disabled, parents with young children
**2** not enough books, books in poor condition, no computers, poor condition of the building
**3** important to have somewhere to study, read newspapers, access Internet, consult reference books; existing sports facilities sufficient

# Unit 4

## Reading, page 28

**CAE Part 3 Multiple choice**

**1** B **2** B **3** D **4** A **5** C **6** A **7** D

## Vocabulary, page 30

**A Adjectives of personality**

| | |
|---|---|
| **1** industrious | **2** slapdash |
| **3** approachable | **4** conceited |
| **5** attentive | **6** single-minded |
| **7** trustworthy | **8** domineering |

**B Time**

| | |
|---|---|
| **1** for | **2** out |
| **3** aside | **4** up |
| **5** of | **6** in |
| **7** at | **8** to |
| **9** on | **10** off |

**C Skills**

*Across:* **8** technical **10** communication **11** personal
*Down:* **1** telephone **2** organizational **3** practical **5** business **6** secretarial **7** managerial **9** language

## Language focus, page 31

**Punctuation**

**1** Since employees
**2** night, profits
**3** doubled.
**4** nights
**5** director, went
**6** explained that
**7** 'Often
**8** Mistry,
**9** accounts department
**10** women.
**11** don't
**12** other's
**13** It's
**14** years, said
**15** However,
**16** now,' he confessed.

## Use of English, page 32

### CAE Part 2 Open cloze

**1** the **2** to
**3** although/though/while/whilst
**4** most **5** has
**6** such **7** in
**8** because/as **9** at
**10** once **11** is
**12** on **13** one
**14** not **15** less

### CAE Part 3 Word formation

**1** representatives
**2** determination
**3** leadership
**4** attendance
**5** applicants
**6** preferred/preferable
**7** competitive
**8** insurance
**9** challenging
**10** receipt

### CAE Part 5 Key word transformations: gerunds and infinitives

**1** refusal to work overtime came
**2** is not/isn't worth (you/your) reading/bothering to read
**3** you like me to carry
**4** made a big/a great/every effort to give
**5** could not/couldn't help laughing
**6** had/'d better leave now or
**7** have difficulty remembering
**8** were made to clean
**9** to him/his being treated

## Writing, page 34

### CAE Part 2 Reports

**2** The correct order and possible headings are:
**4** Introduction
**2** General background
**1** The effect of the car
**5** The effect of television
**3** Future developments

**3**

**Language used to compare the past and the present**
Street games ... are no longer such a common sight.
cycling ... is becoming less attractive
youngsters now spend more time in the home ...
The main difference between now and twenty years ago ...
the increased wealth and greater amount of free time available ...
Where previously whole families ..., now children ...
Courting couples rarely go ballroom dancing ... as they once did; instead ...

**Language used to make future predictions**
Teenagers and people in their twenties may well spend ...
They might even begin to wish ...

**Different ways of referring to young people**
young people
our youth
teenagers and people in their twenties
children
courting couples

**Different ways of referring to free time**
free time
spare time
leisure time

**4**
*but two other developments have restricted the nature and quality of leisure time activities*
*Sadly, youngsters now spend more time in the home*
*they stay in to watch television, or perhaps worse, attend wild pop concerts or parties, where they dance in uncontrolled ways*

**5**
**a** The growth in the popularity of the car
**b** particularly with the construction of motorways
**c** the increased wealth and greater amount of free time available to young people

## Unit 5

### Reading, page 36

**CAE Part 1 Multiple choice**

**1** D **2** A **3** B **4** B **5** C **6** A

### Vocabulary, page 38

**Adjective and noun collocations**

**1**

**1** love
**2** feelings
**3** couple
**4** relationship
**5** friend
**6** family
**7** argument
**8** tension

**2**

**1** love-hate
**2** pointless
**3** unrequited
**4** mixed
**5** immediate
**6** close
**7** courting
**8** social

### Language focus, page 38

**Relative clauses**

**1** who
**2** which
**3** which
**4** whose
**5** where
**6** why
**7** who
**8** that/who

**Alternatives to relative clauses**

**1** Venus and Serena Williams – tennis players (Maud Watson beat her sister Lilian in the first women's final in 1884).
**2** Michael and Ralf Schumacher – Formula 1 racing drivers
**3** The Marx brothers – actors. Groucho (3b), Chico, Harpo, Zeppo and Gummo
**4** Janet and Michael Jackson – popstars. The group was The Jackson 5 (later The Jacksons).
**5** JF and RF Kennedy – US politicians. Robert was himself assassinated while campaigning for the presidency in 1968.

**2**

**1 b** the *one who* collected the winner's trophy
**2 a** a go-kart *which was* powered by a lawnmower engine.
**b** the first *one who phoned* his mother.
**3 a** Monkey Business, Duck Soup and A Night at the Opera, all *of which were* released/*which were* all released in the 1930s.
**b** a moustache *which was* painted on with black greasepaint
**4 a** Fans *who were* hoping to see Janet
**b** a group *which comprised* himself and four of his eight brothers and sisters.
**5 a** the youngest man *who was* ever elected President, he was also the youngest *one who died.*
**b** Robert, *who was* known affectionately as Bobby, had evidence *which backed up/could back up* his suspicions

### Use of English, page 40

**CAE Part 4 Gapped sentences**

**1** fell
**2** strong
**3** took
**4** couple
**5** turn

**CAE Part 1 Multiple-choice cloze**

**1** C **2** B **3** A **4** D **5** B **6** A **7** D
**8** D **9** B **10** C **11** A **12** A

### Writing, page 42

**CAE Part 2 Essay**

**2** The saying means that it is more useful to know the right people than to have knowledge.
**3** b
**4** A
**5 a** 6 **b** 5 **c** 7 **d** 4
**e** 2 **f** 1 **g** 8 **h** 3

# Unit 6

## Reading, page 44

### CAE Part 4 Multiple matching

1

**b** The writer reports what the pupils and teachers have said about Henry (for example: undisputed star/soulful eyes/a pupil's best friend/a super dog/a calming influence etc). She does not use any language to argue or disagree with these descriptions.

2

**1** F **2** D **3** A **4** B **5** C **6** A **7** E **8** D
**9** A **10** B **11** E **12** D **13** G **14** E **15** G

## Vocabulary, page 46

### A Sleep

**1** to **2** up
**3** through **4** into
**5** over **6** on
**7** off **8** from

### B Abilities

**1** d **2** b **3** e **4** a **5** f **6** c

### C Adjectives in film reviews

**1** unconvincing **2** innovative
**3** clichéd **4** gripping
**5** over-hyped **6** moving
**7** excruciating **8** stunning

## Language focus, page 47

1

**1** a **2** b **3** b **4** a **5** b

2

**1** is understood to be planning a takeover bid for its rival
**2** are said (by police) to have taken place on Monday
**3** motorcyclist is believed to have been travelling at over 100 miles per hour
**4** were thought to be/to have been responsible for the outbreak of flu
**5** was alleged to have lied in order to protect her boyfriend
**6** my camera stolen last weekend
**7** to get/have your eyes tested
**8** got my foot stuck in the hole

## Use of English, page 48

### CAE Part 2 Open cloze

**1** being/getting **2** do
**3** who/that **4** only/just/merely
**5** themselves **6** to
**7** is/gets **8** as/being
**9** from **10** with
**11** for/without **12** be/get
**13** Not/Hardly **14** at
**15** while/whilst/when

### CAE Part 3 Word formation

**1** Researchers **2** greatness
**3** variety **4** containing
**5** responses **6** noticeably
**7** recognition **8** unreliable
**9** knowledge **10** preference

## Writing, page 49

### CAE Part 2 Article

1

Version B. Whilst the general content is the same, it is far more interesting to read than A, and the language used is richer and more varied. For example, compare *got good marks, good at sport* and *sports facilities were very good* in version A, with *academic achievement was high, talented young sportsmen* and *extensive sports facilities* in version B. The opening paragraph in B engages the reader's interest and the closing paragraph leaves the reader with something to think about (see 3 B below).

2

**a** Paragraph 3
**b** Paragraphs 1, 2 and 4
**c** Paragraph 1: *the secondary school I had the misfortune to attend*
Paragraph 2: *The teacher was the source of all knowledge* etc
*... trapped in a time bubble of passive learning and iron discipline*
Paragraph 4: the whole paragraph
**d** Paragraph 2: *Whilst the trend up and down the country* etc
Paragraph 3: *Indeed, unlike most other schools at the time ...*

**3**

**A**

**1**

**2** Teaching and learning methods
**3** Discipline
**4** Range of subjects
**5** Academic achievement
**6** Facilities
**7** Extra-curricular activities

**2** All except 'Range of subjects'.

**B**

**1** A quotation from a teacher is used to engage the reader's interest in the first sentence.
Rhetorical questions, followed by a brief answer from the writer, are used in the final paragraph to leave the reader something to think about.

**2**

**1** A fact or statistic
**2** A question
**3** A story
**4** An unusual statement
**5** A comparison

## Unit 7

## Reading, page 52

### CAE Part 2 Gapped text

**1**

**1** = D **2** = E **3** = A **4** = B **5** = G **6** = C
F = not used

**2**

set out – arranged or displayed in writing
set up – started running a business

**3**

**2** b **3** e **4** a **5** g **6** f **7** d

## Vocabulary, page 54

### Phrasal verbs

**1** brought
**2** worn
**3** get
**4** broke
**5** put
**6** come

### Word formation

**1**

| *-en* | *en-* |
|---|---|
| deafen | encourage |
| heighten | endanger |
| deepen | enrich |
| sadden | enforce |
| broaden | |

**2**

**1** heightened **2** deepening
**3** encouraging **4** endangered
**5** enforcement **6** saddened
**7** broadens/broadened, enriches/enriched
**8** deafening

## Language focus, page 55

### Reported speech

**1** The following words should be crossed out:

**1** refused/offered
**2** denied/claimed
**3** accused/complained
**4** persuaded/encouraged
**5** complimented/congratulated
**6** suggested/argued
**7** urge/convince
**8** told/assured
**9** suggested/proposed
**10** ordered/insisted

**2**

**1 a** he would cut
**b** to cut
**2 a** thought I should take
**b** (that) I (should) take/(that) I took
**3 a** they had to leave
**b** them to leave
**4 a** he had always loved
**b** having always loved
**5 a** hadn't stolen it
**b** having stolen it/stealing it
**6 a** was paid
**b** to have been paid
**7 a** she could take
**b** his name should not
**8 a** had been abducted
**b** have been abducted

## Use of English, page 57

### CAE Part 1 Multiple-choice cloze

**1** B **2** D **3** C **4** D **5** A **6** B **7** A
**8** C **9** C **10** D **11** B **12** A

### CAE Part 2 Open cloze

**1** do
**2** are
**3** of
**4** these
**5** for
**6** This/It
**7** either
**8** before
**9** as
**10** not
**11** If
**12** until
**13** only
**14** being
**15** you

## Writing, page 58

### CAE Part 2 Review

**2** Yes

**3**

**1** title
**2** performance
**3** nomination
**4** set
**5** scenes
**6** climax
**7** score
**8** action
**9** insight
**10** lines

**4**

extremely powerful acting performance
well-deserved Oscar nomination
the boxing scenes are entirely convincing
(the film builds up to) a dramatic climax
(Michael Mann's) expert direction
the moving musical score
(one of the most) memorable moments (of the film)
(it provides) a fascinating insight (into)
witty lines

**5**

is reason enough to see the film
don't be put off if you're not a boxing fan
There's something for everyone in the film
will have you laughing out loud

# Unit 8

## Reading, page 60

### CAE Part 3 Multiple choice

**1**

**1** D **2** D **3** C **4** A **5** C **6** B **7** D

**2**

**1** c **2** a **3** b

**3**

**1** H **2** D **3** H **4** H **5** D

**4**

**a** underhand
**b** devious
**c** reputable
**d** candid
**e** straight

## Vocabulary, page 62

### Verbs formed with *up, down, over* and *under*

**1**

**1** uphear
**2** overgo
**3** underroot
**4** uprule
**5** downhold

**2**

**1** uphold, overrule
**2** undergo
**3** update, upgrade
**4** undercut
**5** downplay

### Adjectives formed with *in, off, on, out* and *over*

**1** oncoming
**2** ongoing
**3** outlying
**4** off-duty
**5** inborn

### Plans

**1**

**1** emergency
**2** devious
**3** impracticable
**4** carry out
**5** put forward
**6** shelve

**2**

**1** impracticable
**2** emergency
**3** devious
**4** shelved
**5** carrying out
**6** put forward

### Computer technology

**1**

**A**

**1 c** mouse mat
**2 d** keyboard
**3 a** laptop
**4 e** disk drive
**5 b** webcan

**B**

**1 d** chat room
**2 e** home page
**3 a** search engine
**4 c** service provider
**5 b** bulletin board

**2**

mouse mat 6
keyboard 8
laptop 1
disk drive 9
webcam 2
chat room 3
home page 10
search engine 5
service provider 7
bulletin board 4

## Language focus, page 64

### Talking about the future

**1** C **2** C **3** B **4** C **5** D **6** C **7** A **8** B

### Determiners

**1** no other
**2** every other
**3** Every few
**4** another two
**5** quite a few/quite a lot of
**6** quite some
**7** not much
**8** some three

## Use of English, page 65

### CAE Part 2 Open cloze

**1** the
**2** of
**3** a
**4** over
**5** them
**6** into
**7** for
**8** Although/Though/While/Whilst/Whereas
**9** by
**10** that/which
**11** its
**12** us
**13** to
**14** at
**15** on/upon

### CAE Part 3 Word formation

**1** undergone
**2** undoubtedly/doubtlessly
**3** functional
**4** inaccuracy/inaccuracies
**5** significant
**6** irresistibly
**7** threatening
**8** compulsively
**9** tendency
**10** productivity/production

### CAE Part 4 Gapped sentences

**1** well
**2** run
**3** odd
**4** medium
**5** purpose

# Unit 9

## Reading, page 68

### CAE Part 1 Multiple choice

**1** B **2** D **3** B **4** A **5** D **6** D

## Vocabulary, page 70

### Doing things alone

**1** c **2** g **3** f **4** d **5** b **6** a **7** h **8** e

### Criticism

**1**

**1** constructive
**2** valid
**3** upset by
**4** arouse
**5** respond to
**6** draw

**2**

**1** A **2** B **3** D **4** C

### Word formation

**1**

**1** composure
**2** hardship
**3** supporting
**4** identity
**5** entry

**2**

**1** winning entry
**2** Supporting Actress
**3** a case of mistaken identity
**4** regained his composure
**5** caused considerable hardship

## Language focus, page 71

### Creating emphasis

**1**

**1** have
**2** what
**3** because
**4** and
**5** it
**6** so

## Use of English, page 72

### CAE Part 1 Multiple-choice cloze

**1** B **2** B **3** D **4** C **5** D **6** C
**7** B **8** B **9** A **10** B **11** B **12** D

### CAE Part 2 Open Cloze

1 could/would
2 little/no
3 on
4 those
5 for
6 with
7 that/which/to
8 Even
9 as
10 unless
11 such
12 By
13 can
14 in
15 since

### CAE Part 3 Word formation

1 safety
2 handful
3 consultant
4 enabled
5 freedom
6 uninhibited
7 cooperative
8 readily
9 deterrent
10 temptation

### CAE Part 5 Key word transformations

1 only when we were in/reached the
2 is all (that) Steve ever talks
3 wasn't/was not until we ('d/had) arrived
4 he did was (to) send
5 soon as she had handed
6 and I took to each
7 disastrous (that) I couldn't/could not wait
8 have/get a tent to

## Writing, page 75

### CAE Part 1 Report

**2**

1 F: successful answers build on the information given in the input, as long as the points added are relevant. eg say why students enjoyed the social events so much, give examples of topics for the cultural talks, and so on.

2 T: and other plans might also be acceptable eg including one or more recommendations in each section (Social events, Cultural events and Weekend excursions).

3 F: the inclusion of headings is a useful and sometimes desirable way of organizing ideas in reports.

4 T: see page 221 of the Grammar reference in the Coursebook for the grammar of *recommend, advise* and *suggest*

5 T: perhaps the most usual register for a report is a formal one, but this is not an absolute requirement for this particular task. Consistency of register, however, is a requirement for all reports.

# Unit 10

## Reading, page 76

### CAE Part 1 Multiple matching

**1**

1 C 2 D 3 A 4 B 5 C 6 B 7 D 8 B
9 C 10 D 11 A 12 B 13 C 14 D 15 A

**2**

1 come(s) first
2 comes to
3 came to a head
4 come and go
5 coming to an end

## Vocabulary, page 78

**1**

| A | B |
|---|---|
| 1 owl | 1 stomach |
| 2 mouse | 2 leaves |
| 3 bee | 3 drum |
| 4 dog | 4 music |
| 5 lion | 5 floorboards |

**2**

1 C 2 A 3 B 4 D 5 D
6 B 7 D 8 A 9 B 10 D

## Language focus, page 79

### Participle clauses

1 'Lord of the Rings: Return of the King' won 11 Oscars, *equalling* the record held by 'Ben Hur' and 'Titanic' for the highest number of Academy Awards.

2 *Having* finally *discovered* where the leak was, we called in a plumber.

3 The school now has 1,254 students, *representing* a 6% increase on last year's figure.

4 Part of the stadium roof collapsed, *injuring* six spectators.

5 *Not being* a parent, I can take my holidays whenever I like.

6 The team has had a disastrous season so far, *winning/having won* only three of its last sixteen games.

7 Our parents *having gone* away for the weekend, my brother and I had a party.

8 *Walking* home from school yesterday, I bumped into Alex.

## Use of English, page 79

### CAE Part 3 Word formation

**1** guaranteed **2** Costing
**3** fitted **4** uninterrupted
**5** luxurious **6** equipped
**7** running **8** breathtaking
**9** sunset **10** permission

### CAE Part 1 Multiple-choice cloze

**1** C **2** D **3** A **4** A **5** B **6** C
**7** D **8** D **9** C **10** A **11** C **12** C

### CAE Part 4 Gapped sentences

**1** complete **2** right
**3** bound **4** show
**5** make

### CAE Part 5 Key word transformations

**1** wishing/wanting to let down
**2** come to/made/taken/reached the/a decision to
**3** (that) you keep an eye on *or* keeping an eye on
**4** more likely you are to suffer
**5** be (of) no use to
**6** came as no surprise to James
**7** is bound to be a change
**8** longer pride themselves on/take pride in

## Writing, page 82

### CAE Part 2 Contribution to a brochure

**2**

*These are generally situated well away from busy towns* to end of paragraph
*can pay as little as 300 Euros for a week in the high season*
*but accommodates up to six people*
*If comfort is a major factor*
*with all the benefits of a five-star hotel* to end of paragraph
*if you really want to pamper yourself*

**3**

*In the lower price bracket*
*Prices vary depending on*
*can pay as little as 300 Euros*
*A rather more expensive option is*
*works out at about 90 Euros*
*money is no object*
*at the upper end of the price range*
*costing anywhere between 150 and 300 Euros*

**4**

offering, designed, depending, located, costing

# Unit 11

## Reading, page 84

### CAE Part 4 Multiple matching

**1**

**1** B **2** D **3** A **4** C **5** B **6** C **7** D **8** B
**9** C **10** A **11** E **12** D **13** E **14** A **15** E

**2**

*Where more than one answer is given, the first of these is the one that appears in the reading text.*

### A Collocations

**1** period/time **2** home/ease
**3** memory **4** word
**5** way

### B Phrasal verbs

**1** to **2** up
**3** on/along **4** out
**5** up

## Vocabulary, page 86

### Sight

**1** visibility **2** eyesight, vision
**3** eye **4** look
**5** sight **6** full
**7** closer **8** naked
**9** keep **10** catch

### Read and write

**1**

**1** off **2** up **3** out **4** into

**2**

**a** 4 **b** 2 **c** 1 **d** 3

## Language focus, page 87

### Inversion

**1**

**1** no **2** have
**3** are **4** but
**5** Not **6** Under
**7** when/if **8** will/can
**9** Only **10** On

**2**

*Possible answers*

**1** had I got **2** she saw
**3** have I had **4** will I allow
**5** had he started **6** did I think
**7** will I follow **8** did they realize

## Use of English, page 88

### CAE Part 4 Gapped sentences

**1** concern
**2** called
**3** account
**4** need
**5** fine

### CAE Part 3 Word formation

**1** environmental **2** specialized/specialised
**3** depth **4** insight
**5** perceptions **6** written
**7** advising **8** encourages/encouraged
**9** inspiration **10** independent

### CAE Part 1 Multiple-choice cloze

**1** A **2** C **3** B **4** D **5** A **6** B
**7** C **8** C **9** A **10** D **11** B **12** C

## Writing, page 90

### CAE Part 2 Information sheet

**1**
**a** Do your homework
**b** Practice makes perfect
**c** The day of the interview

**2**
**1** The best place to look is
**2** It's also worthwhile to
**3** it's far more advisable to
**4** Make a special point of rehearsing
**5** It would be a mistake to
**6** it's always wise to

**3**

**A Gathering ideas**

**i**
**1** Listening
**2** Vocabulary, Grammar
**3** Reading, Vocabulary, Writing, Speaking
**4** Writing
**5** Speaking

**ii**
*Answers will vary.*

**B Organizing ideas**
**b** would be inappropriate

# Unit 12

## Reading, page 92

### CAE Part 2 Gapped text

**1**
**1** = G **2** = E **3** = B **4** = F **5** = C **6** = A
**D** = not used

**2**
**1** tap, sparkling **2** drinking
**3** rain **4** salt
**5** running **6** flood

## Vocabulary, page 94

### Verb and noun collocations

**1**
**1** hidden treasure **2** housework
**3** someone a favour **4** an effort
**5** a lie **6** birth

**2**
**1** pay, attention **2** kept, promise
**3** welcomed, decision **4** wish, harm
**5** lead, life **6** meet, expectations
**7** kept, temper **8** meet, deadline
**9** made, mind **10** wish, luck

### Approximation

**1** something **2** so
**3** Very **4** Just
**5** round **6** upwards
**7** some **8** something

## Language focus, page 95

### Conjunctions

*Possible answers*
**1** I enjoyed the film *Ali* even though I don't like boxing.
**2** They won the game despite the fact that two of their players were sent off.
**3** We'd better/We ought to phone her, otherwise she'll worry about us.
**4** However I comb it, my hair always looks a mess!
**5** I'll leave the plate there in case you want some more later.
**6** We spoke very quietly so as not to wake up my dad.

### Modal verbs

**1** permitted **2** forbidden
**3** recommended **4** required
**5** obliged **6** supposed
**7** presumed **8** obligatory

## Use of English, page 96

### CAE Part 3 Word formation

1 knowledge
2 discovery
3 intensifies
4 erosion
5 unreliable
6 threatened
6 ecological
8 endangered
9 survival
10 sponsorship

### CAE Part 2 Open cloze

1 not
2 what
3 across/around/round/over
4 until
5 there
6 which
7 any
8 to
9 With
10 only
11 after/following
12 but
13 so
14 without
15 the

### CAE Part 4 Gapped sentences

1 draw
2 credit
3 come
4 approach
5 lead

### CAE Part 5 Key word transformations

1 him (all) the best for
2 up studying/his studies met with
3 let her know in
4 in case the shops run/sell
5 otherwise tigers/the tiger could/may/might die/ be wiped
6 not knowing/speaking a single word/bit of
7 unless he made more (of an)
8 never to have lent

## Writing, page 98

### CAE Part 2 Proposal

**1**

1 This has led to
2 therefore
3 also
4 instead
5 Whilst
6 As well as
7 Clearly
8 Finally
9 In order to
10 as

**2**

*a substantial proportion of the budget should therefore be allocated to*
*money might also be spent on*
*funds would also need to be set aside for*
*some of the budget should be devoted to*

## Unit 13

## Reading, page 100

### CAE Part 2 Gapped text

**1**

1 = E 2 = G 3 = B 4 = F 5 = D 6 = C
A = not used

**2**

1 revival
2 descriptions
3 publication
4 pronouncement
5 expectations
6 turnover
7 enthusiasts
8 anxiety

## Vocabulary, page 102

### Phrasal verbs and prepositions

**A Eating and drinking**

1 off 2 down 3 at 4 up

**B Deception**

1 into 2 on 3 at 4 for

### Expressions with *eat*

**1**

1 home
2 hand
3 profits
4 words
5 horse
6 bird

**2**

2 a 3 f 4 b 5 e 6 d

### Intensifiers

1 b 2 e 3 f 4 h 5 d 6 a 7 g 8 c

## Language focus, page 103

### Comparisons

1 … I worked as a security guard …
2 … attracted her to him as/but his warm …
3 … anywhere near as hard …
4 … a great deal more convenient …
5 … the film was so hugely successful …
6 … the same way as certain types …

## Use of English, page 104

### CAE Part 1 Multiple-choice cloze

1 C 2 C 3 D 4 D 5 C 6 A
7 B 8 A 9 B 10 C 11 D 12 C

**CAE Part 2 Open cloze**

| | |
|---|---|
| **1** up | **2** out |
| **3** to | **4** with |
| **5** they | **6** into |
| **7** them | **8** as |
| **9** while/whilst | **10** has |
| **11** of | **12** as |
| **13** are | **14** to |
| **15** no | |

**CAE Part 3 Word formation**

| | |
|---|---|
| **1** gathering | **2** imaginative |
| **3** proof | **4** unattractive |
| **5** refreshingly | **6** creatively |
| **7** combinations | **8** heights |
| **9** encouraging | **10** fussiest |

**CAE Part 4 Gapped sentences**

| | |
|---|---|
| **1** scare | **2** range |
| **3** go | **4** forward |
| **5** cover | |

# Unit 14

## Reading, page 108

**CAE Part 1 Multiple choice**

**1** C **2** B **3** D **4** C **5** B **6** A

**2b**

**a** scamper
**b** stumble
**c** dwindle
**d** plead
**e** pat

## Vocabulary, page 110

**Money**

**1** counterfeit
**2** pocket
**3** housekeeping
**4** ransom
**5** redundancy
**6** sponsorship

**Verbs usually associated with money**

**1**

**1** C **2** B **3** C **4** A **5** D

**2**

| | |
|---|---|
| **1** pay | **2** owe |
| **3** lend | **4** save |
| **5** borrow | |

**3**

| | |
|---|---|
| **1** owe, an apology | **2** pay, respects |
| **3** borrowed, word | **4** owed, a favour |
| **5** paying, a compliment | |

## Language focus, page 111

**Noun phrases**

**1**

| | |
|---|---|
| **1** sign | **2** matter |
| **3** grain, pack | **4** sense |
| **5** state | **6** source |
| **7** depths, height | **8** chances |

**2**

| | |
|---|---|
| **1** can of beer | **2** door handle |
| **3** a scrap of evidence | **4** pieces of advice |
| **5** three-page essay | **6** a week's work |
| **7** mountain tops | **8** last April's edition |

## Use of English, page 112

**CAE Part 2 Open cloze**

| | |
|---|---|
| **1** if/though | **2** to |
| **3** there | **4** in |
| **5** once, when, immediately, as | |
| **6** one | **7** of |
| **8** out | **9** is |
| **10** spite | **11** being |
| **12** on | **13** what |
| **14** of/for/with | **15** their |

**CAE Part 3 Word formation**

| | |
|---|---|
| **1** deception/deceit | **2** contestant |
| **3** winning | **4** trial |
| **5** numerous | **6** persistent |
| **7** unsure | **8** strategically |
| **9** recording | **10** dishonesty |

**CAE Part 5 Key word transformations**

**1** it if you paid in *or* it if you would/could pay in
**2** to be no sign of
**3** as an invasion of
**4** chances of survival/surviving are thought
**5** had felt/had a sense of achievement
**6** wanting to be the centre of
**7** ten-day camping trip would do
**8** with a regular source/means

## Writing, page 114

**Key vocabulary**

**Task 1**

**1**

**1** c **2** e **3** a **4** b **5** d

**2**

**1** Tiles
**2** Power lines
**3** Families
**4** Roads
**5** Crops

**Task 2**

**1** installed **b**
**2** pedestrianized **e**
**3** demolished **d**
**4** built **a**
**5** introduced **c**

**Task 3**

**1** warm
**2** spend
**3** wait
**4** maintain
**5** begin

**Task 4**

**1** life
**2** control
**3** debts
**4** source
**5** demand